REMNANTS

JANE BURN
BOB BEAGRIE

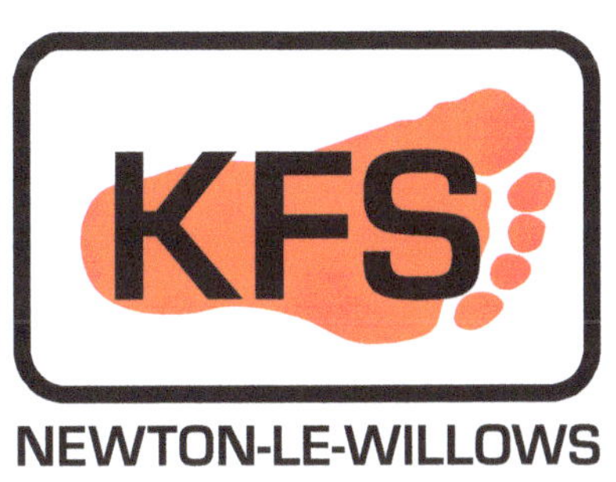

Published in the United Kingdom in 2019
by The Knives Forks And Spoons Press,
51 Pipit Avenue,
Newton-le-Willows,
Merseyside,
WA12 9RG.

ISBN 978-1-912211-35-7

Acknowledgements:

Bob Beagrie:

'Vela' was first published in the *Heavenly Bodies Anthology* (Beautiful Dragons Press 2014),
'Slow Recovery' first published in the chapbook *Nobody* (Hunting Raven Press, 2017),
'Searim Seothra' first published in the *Intercity Flow Anthology* (Ek Zuban 2015),
'Amanita Muscaria' first published in *Northbound* (Vane Women Press 2016).

'Versions of: Remants', 'Crusoe Recycled', 'Vela', 'Wolfling', 'My Grandmother's Ghost', 'Amanita Muscaria', 'Slow Recovery' and 'Searim Seothra' have been developed into recorded soundscapes by Project Lono and can be listened to at https://soundcloud.com/projectlono-1

Jane Burn:

'Oldfriend Woman' first published in *The Rialto,*
'If I believed in him like I should' first published in *Ground: Poetry, Faith and Doubt,*
'Head at the Window' first published in *The Rialto,*
'Life in Ogham' first published in *The Rialto,*
'My Dawtie' winner of the Silver Wyvern in the 2018 Poetry on the Lake Open Competition,
'Viaticum' first published in *The Rialto,*
'Human Rubble' first published in *The Cantebury Poet of the Year Anthology*, 2014,
'Haruspex' first published in *The Black Light Engine Room Magazine*,
'Island of Kings' first published in *The Black Light Engine Room Magazine,*
'Hamrammr' first published on *The Learned Pig*.

'images on pages 19,47, 51 by Bob Beagrie, images on pages 15,24,28,45,52,63,69, 84 by Jane Burn'

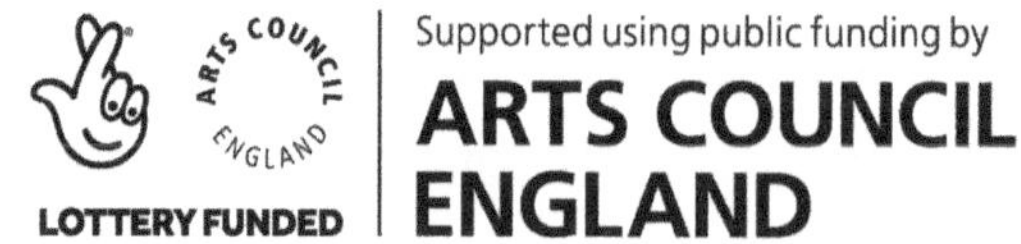

Contents:

The past, like the future, is indefinite and exists only as a spectrum of possibilities.

–Stephen Hawking

Remnants

The Old Man ysed t' tac us oot onte the rocks
snot-slippy n' green at doon-tide n' lathered
wi' flies that foggled awer feet as we stepped
leery over the wyrm-stems o' knotted kelp
te peer inte them rock pools, picking winkles,
ousting stones te latch them scuttling crabs;
the sea rose n' fell aboot us, baring n' covering
the boles o' a petrified forest, the limpited ridge-tiles
of a once thriving B & B called Neptune View,
the washed-oot bingo hall, the barnacled spire
of an ainchent kirk where the One God
once drooned. 'hlisten', he telled us,
'Sumetymes ye can harcen the kirk bells
still ringing undra the waves, calling all the Mer.'
At niyht I'd wayke, thinkin I'd heard 'em,
te pry awer ower stockade o' scrap cars n' cawld stores
across the flood playn n' wunder if the Mer
we're gatherin' te march fro the deep watters
bringing the cawld fury o' the Drooned God
upon the remnants o' the bairns o' men.
Efrey morning, for me learnings, the Old Man
had me recite the songs n' psalms the Olders sang
on board ship throughoot thor Greet Floating:
The Rhapsody o' the Hrafen Skull
The Ballad o' the Boar's Tusc
The Hymn o' the Stag's Heart
The Canticle o' the Whale's Lung.

The Pre-Flood Patriarch

I, I have this antediluvian ache. *I, I* have swum a long time – longly,
deeply, ages since before the flood, before the end of the first world.
I, I was there at *Creation* even before the time when the *Great He* said
let there be light, and the seeing of this light was good. *Let there be*

a Great Floating, and the knowledge of this wash was as true as the sky
He laid above me. Back, in times when there was only void and *I, I* was
dust, floating bits of beginning, until the hands of He made good
their gather and stitch. Put me in order, formed me loose, swirled me

upon the surface of his new-built orb in generous abandon. For the first
time, *I, I* was pulse and swell, was a taster of salt. The sheer acres of me,
there was no ordering my wondrous self. He, the *Beggetter Of Things,*
All-Seer, ever watchful saw he must curb my undulence – too much of the flesh

about me, too much curve. *Let there be an expanse in the midst of the waters.*
Sand to split me, break my skin, make me watch my step. Wherever I am,
I, I must be fettered to the moon, caught, corralled, controlled. Pulled back
'ere I get too settled on my shores, get my foamy clutch too much in land.

The Deluge

i)

I am woman, cast to Earth
when my mother ate what she should not.
Be happy, thou naked things
sayeth the Lord of all the Garden.
Ask not for more than what I
have placed here for prettification,
simple glorification –
be satisfied. I have given you
great things. Plentitudes of fruit,
honey, nectar, flowers, all good stuffs.
But the apple. Red as lips
suffused by sin, red as bloodshed, red
as shepherd's morning. Polished
as a lake, tempting as ice in heat.
Elohim saw her waist, saw
its hinge as she bent it to reach,
saw her marvellous breasts swing,
ripe as damsons, small bulbs of her spine
knuckling beneath sugary skin.
Her arm unrolled in soft tendril, hand out,
fingers seeking, cupping, pluck.

ii)

The Gibborim desired us, Eve's wastrels. Holy, them, yet anxious
for a taste from the apple of us, wanting what they are meant to be
above the wanting of. Giant as the sky, mouths the size of fisher-boats,
they make our little forms into a fascination. Twiddle us in their fingers,
run their mammoth tongues round blubbered rims, slick us in greasy
glances, eat us with their eyes. I am bathing, sea-swum, stilled in my
floatatious contemplation of the moon-struck empyrean lid – the lipped
wet is a silken feel of ticklement on my skin. I see this flying thing,
purling above – bat? Bird? More than owl, yet I decipher feathers –
I see the kick of human legs, the reach of human arms, the point
of a finger, right at me, as if to say *Thou!* No nakedity, for he is gown'd
and clad in finest swathes of this and that. It is a Fallen Angel, He-Sprite,
fluttering Man Thing, *Tell me*, I husk to the foul of his golden ear.
Thou who art so righteous – whose will be the Original Sin?

Pieta

God is Golden. Humble eyes blinking, reverential.
Others gawp, all jackdaw with the shiny, illuminated while
they peer at gilded halleluiahs. Always someone reeling off
a childhood thread of half-remembered Sunday knowledge;
wasn't there something about rich men and needles?
Angels bearing up their halos, heads in pools of yellow light –
temples palmed as if they would explode with *Holy! Holy!*

The Gospels talk in shades of precious metal, inked encaustic,
Lord Almighty cried into curlicues – sepia tears from slanted nibs.
Scribing, finger-cold yet warmed in heart by such devotions,
the cell bound faithful daubed their lac onto majesty. Wreathed
foil round frowning seraph faces – puffed skewings from tips
of genuflecting fingers, from the emaciated cheekbones of Christ.
A fainted Messiah, thinned by the scrape of lunarium blades,

shaded green-earth in his bridge of bones, skin pulled tight
across his pitied death. Painting the Virgin blue of Mother,
swathed in smalted robes, the pain of Annunciation. *Woman,*
behold your son! Burnished with prayer, the crafter wipes
the pumice – *You turn man back into dust*. Our skies are bound
with stars, jewels spinning in heaven, high above us. Souls
lamenting *you are gone; yet I remember Your name in the night.*

The Rhapsody of the Hrafen's Skull

i)

Delicate in death, its two parts
form a perfect fit, a fluted tune

the bulbous cavern of the brain-pan
recalls how to coast blind winds

two slender jaw bones are the strings
of a mandolin stretched in stream lines

to the sharp, savage sweep of the beak
that tore flesh and grated hunger

from a boding groan to nerve rending
krazo to tear gallows light in two

stretching quavers across syrinxes –
now caws in cold, white quietude.

ii)

Orebh. Orebh, the ruffled shadow
skulking amid thick yew gloom

Prince of Plunderers, blue-black
snatcher of cold stilled sight

perched at the helm from charcoaled
dawn long into skid-marked night

as the drowned waved their winning
scratch cards the Deluge swallowed

sky and land in blinding flashes
in sodden sheets, in folds of gales.

iii)

An eye of bled ink piercing torrents
to a city gnawing its own skeleton,

blossoms of rust in flood where sunken
street lights still blink beneath,

still dance in shimmers
of deep drum and bass –

it knows survival's price, first to
leave the ship to roam white crests

in search of a freshly formed beach
littered with tide's abandoned fruit,

a feast for the soot throated screecher
flapping round the heels of the Reaper

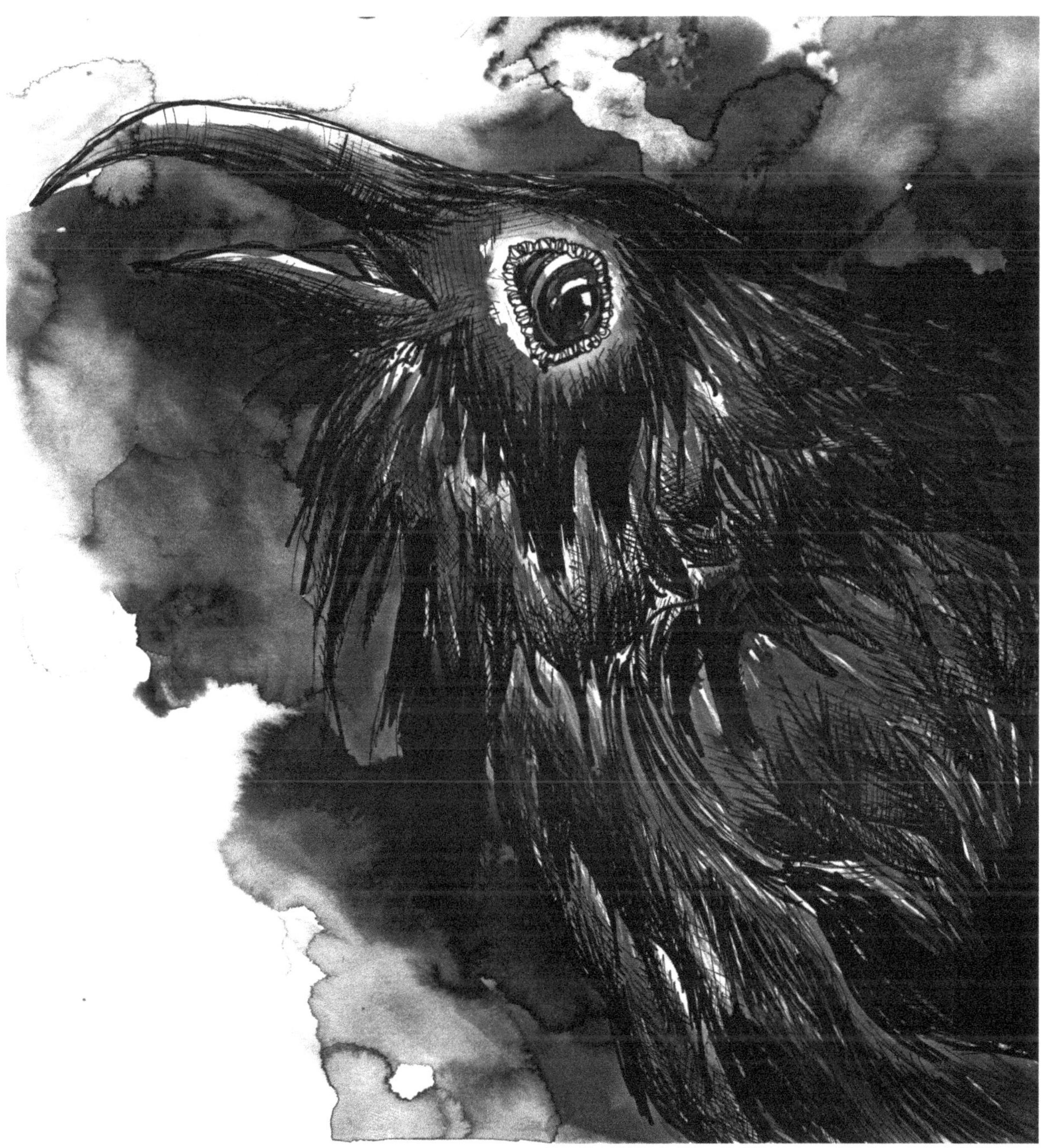

Gedeon says to Oreb

I hear you, glass-eye, bodied to a slick bud, closed
up on that tree – burnt magnolia pseudo terminal.

I hear you, throat tight as cocked movement,
waiting to crack that voice into dawn ears,

cawk the break of day in gravelled yak. *I hear you,*
rasping claw on bough, shuffling barbs. From where

I stand, you are a blot. I am a feller of trees. You
reach your wings to the wind, carry the gaudy haloes

of the sun upon them in a mockery of God. *Beth-ba'-ra*
whispers, *I will claim you again*. You make your flight

above mountains of cut plough – I see the hills of Ephraim
in the glazed chop of their mountained sides. Your beak

will seam with rot, thou feaster of dead things, scourer, picker
of dead flesh. *I see you,* tatter of shreds, up-chucked into a frame

of the Almighty's fog-whiffed sky. *I see you,* day liver
of night chill – head a tissue of bird-bones like the stiffened shell

of a byssus glove. *I see you* vanish into the rustled green
of tree-thick. Fleece, snatched on wired fencing carries

the wet of dew, the grass bears the same. You will be delivered,
scrappy rag-thing. Him that knows has promised me that.

I am no man-crow, Destroyer

I am nursing this clutch inside of me. Three,
maybe four,
maybe one.
Morrigan, one foot in the world of the living,
one in the world of the dead.
Ill-luck bringer, me, to those who think themselves
above the Gods –
Thou shalt shoulder me before too long has passed and know
that I come, to guide thee to the Underworld.
Him of the *riastrad*, born of Lugh could not master me
and such men as this were what made myth.
So get thee gone, Gid'on – thou art not here, in
judgement o'er me.
The bitumen of my wings is clung to the atmosphere as I
fly –
I see you, eyeballing my smear. Your flaming sword
of salvation
is war, done to rid the world of Pagan prayer.
My sisters wait for me in the deep woods – Mother
made us fit for battle. The cough of our song
is a tune fit for a Samhain tryst. Dagda waits
to sow the seeds that I bring in handfuls of blood.
My love
is a river – if you should place one foot there, it
will wash you,
wash that Almighty, all-consuming thing from your head –
leave you suppurating at my hooked toes.
And all over,
the World will know that not even thee, in your might
could resist this stuff of Legends – give up your
Glorifications.
I am making the skulls of my children – within me are their
little lives,
the treasure of their future souls.
I could turn you to water, I could make a puddle of you,
dip my beak and drink. Call on Badb and Macha to sup
the same, swell their craws upon thy death.

Foraging the Weightless

The shifting waffe o' her face
on the farrside o' the fyre
squinting in swirls o' smoke –
a single glance, caught, cast off

The gobble-racket o' geese
leaving the strand te seek
another summer insumother
place thor wings waft flames

o' me niyht dreams –
her singing as she forages
barefoot
along shrinking tidelines

We make use o' whatever
we find, reinvent the world
with salvage, grow a new Eden
from sea-swept fragments

o' the Badtymes

She's a carrier bag whipped
up by the stray wind,
a lone goose feather stuck
inte slow drying sand.

I'm afeared the gusts will come
to sweep her across the waves

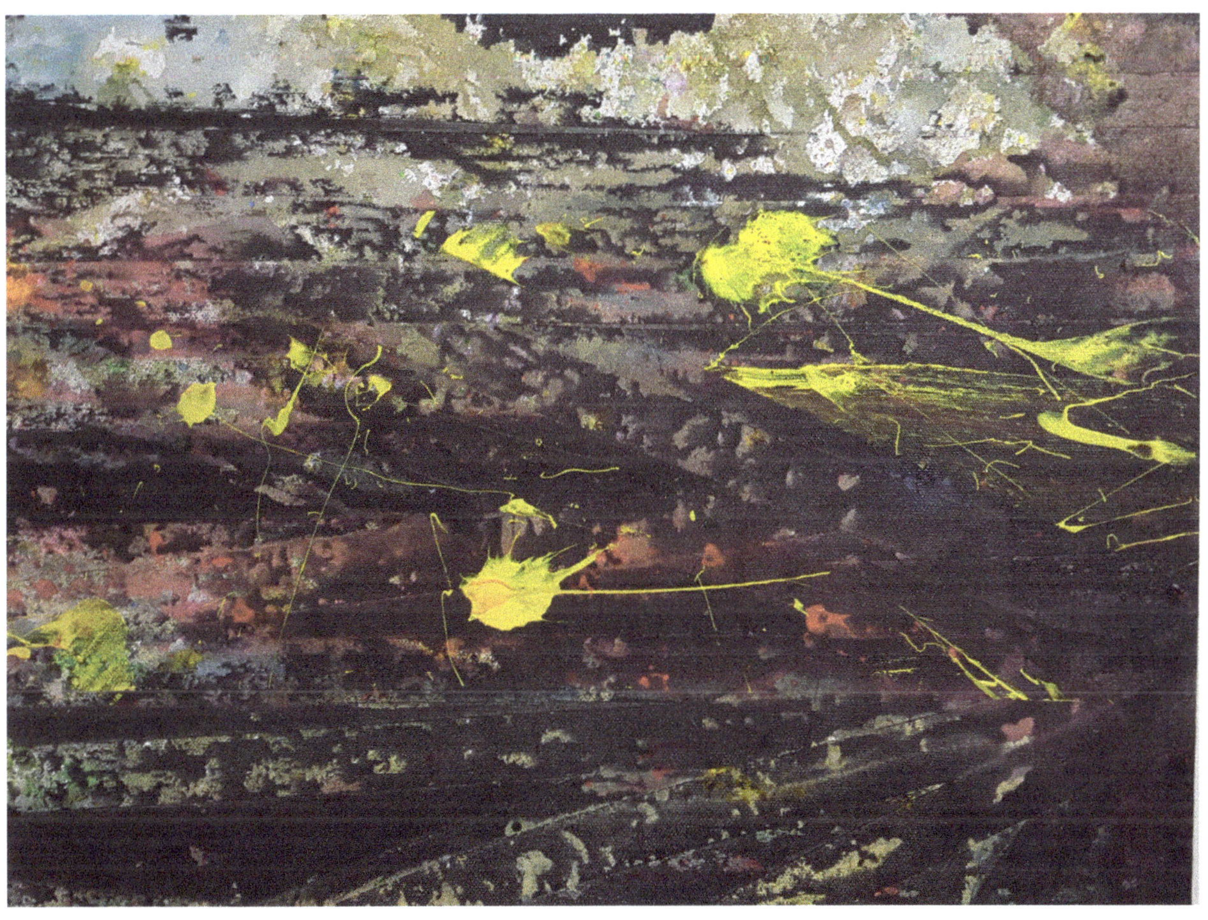

The Nephilim Speaks

Alpha, Omega – He was there at the formation
    of dust and particles, He was there
at the bringing of land and sea. He is here now,
    and will be at the end of it all. And yet
I see her, this remnant of Eve's garden

    and she is lost to lamentation. Woe I see
in her akimbo form on the back of the sea –
    I smell her sadness through the salt air.
The way her face is an unscribed egg, this oval,
    two sockets, blank beneath the blinking.

I wonder if she wishes the waves
    to take her. O! Do not tempt damnation
with this throwing away of self! Yea, do not
    risk to bear the wrath of this young God –
he is strong in His vengefulness.

    Her soul is tangible, it is phosphorescent.
I lower myself, vortex of wing and limb –
    she, she is the first of these Daughters
that has drawn me down. I am unsure
    of what she will feel to touch – we Immortals

are built of feather and wind, fear and ache.
    I do not know the feel of flesh –
reach my length of arm, hand, finger out. Scoop her,
    as a gatherer would a bundle of sticks –
she whispers, almost beyond my ken and I

    pretend not to hear. I want to tell her
that all this *he begat her, begat him, begat them,*
    begat whom will be a thing of the past,
ere too long. Your gabbling kind will die,
    will drown their din in a rush and *Jared, Enoch,*

Seth, Lamech, Kenan, Adam, Enos, Mahalalel,
Methuselah and all their kin will
be gone in water. This is a Happening and I would
take her where it would be not.
I could tell her, that in the future there will be

spectacles – Howard Hughes will love aeroplanes,
Church will be a Sunday thing. Her kind
will tuck in alleyways, make their own
Armageddons, seek fulfilment in shoes.
As I carry her, she hums, light and thin.

The sound is bird keen, her eyes are veiled
with the silk cockle of her lids and I do
not know if she is beautiful, in the way humans measure
these imperceptible things. I will fall
to Earth with her, if she will have me there.

Ascension

Since I were elected PATRUM
the sea is nowt but a murmur –

a pebble swathed in leather
locked wi' its scent
in a bottomless drawer,

it is singing te the sky
scraping itself 'gainst earth
a stone rolling over a tomb

Since I took the seat
the moon has not looked on me

no toad has croaked
at me passing shadow

me nails 'ave curled inte spirals
me hair they pleat wi' seal oil
an' shells as I pretend te sleep

I am filled by the urge to eat dirt

But me feet, hands, me lips
shan't feel its wonder-squelch
nor its gritcrumblerun

afore the day all feeling flees
this flesh-sail like a Luna Moth
abandoning its cocoon.

Until then I step only on blossom
to ward off THE DEVASTASHUN

Wyrm

Helminth – I eet myn way into holes, up thurgh layers of erthe.
Soukynge out burrows. I am telling how I digged adoun to Hell
and alle ways up again! I went a thousand fathmes deep,

hearde the loothly revelrye of careyne-cows –'twas full of moans.
Those feends, souls all struck with woodnesse and thonder-dent.
Poor forpyned goosts! The devil abideth, girt in cloaks

embrouded up with Baphomets, curling horns of goots, hedde apiked
with gleedes, saucefleem visage full of shadwe. Hands all shiten,
crunching wang-tooths on their mary-bones, deve to their wo.

Derknesse – hem caytyves in all their freletee, mouths all chewed
on mullock, thick with lith. Fir, hir fel to brenne, brymstoon shour
and ryvers foul. I was aferd and axed them *canstow tell the way*

to reach mo hooly mede? I ysene ynough of yvel. Blent, they were;
so silent when I quod wher finds I Heavene? Noon of hem koude seye.
Hem quod *perhaps there is no God. Never it did we trowe*.

I did astert – I used my konnyng, raughte for eir and turned away
from heete. Daswen in the light, I herde the soun of trompe, saugh
the sovereyn trone – the gras of egre aungels, biwreyed as cleere as sonne.

Them weep and rowned *namo teeres! We the wayk warente.*
noon are wemelees that clepeth at the chirche dore. I am ham!
I will myn abluicions werche on the soil –

myn teeres are myn biheeste, myn aleyes are myn portehors.
If wyrms had knows I would have er kneled to hym –
Deus hic, deus hic, alderlevest Kyng!

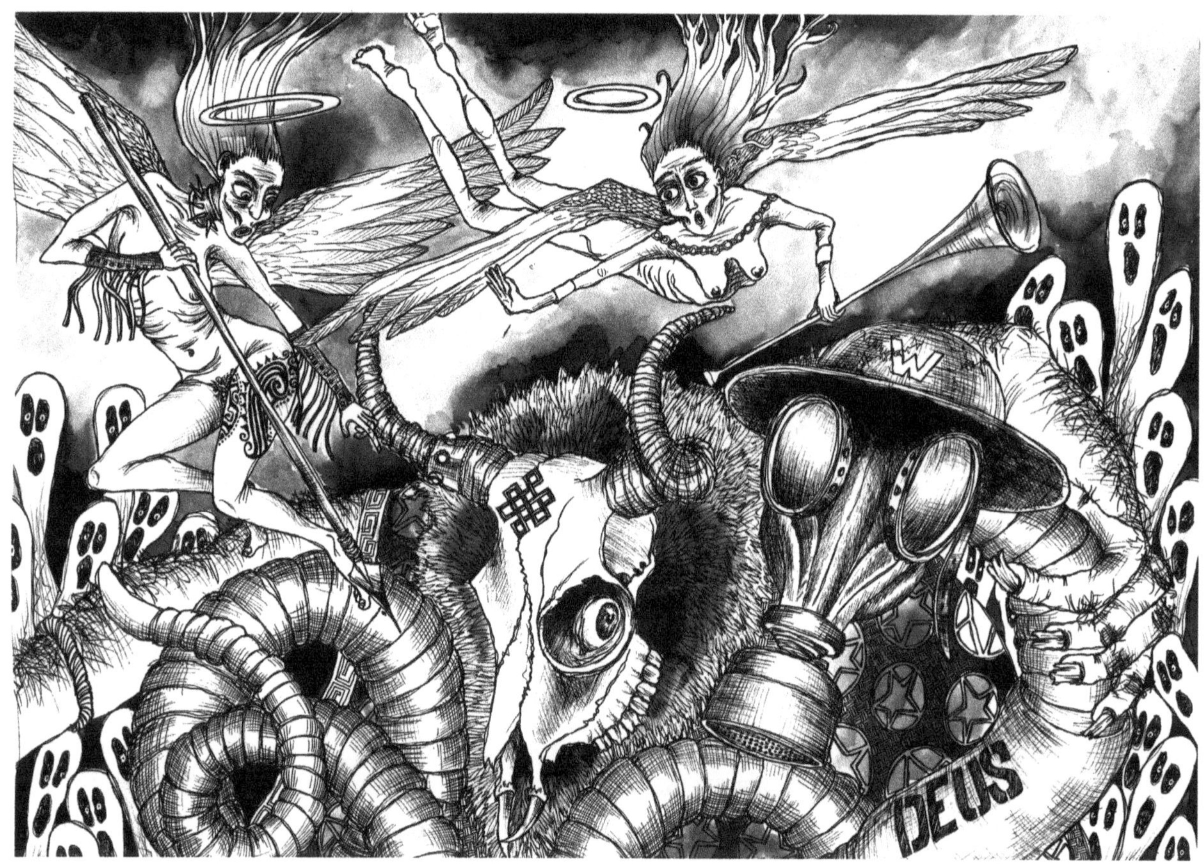
W
DEUS

Desert Mother

Amma, they bid me. *Tell us of the old time*. Unravelling
my Coptic tongue, I do my best to make a wonderland
of this waste. Wind sifts the sand into a pretence of mist –

I give myself to rememberings of salt-shore sea fog,
mercury and diamonds on my skin, in the dawn. I came
from ripples, my father with his kelp-wrought head,

tither of shells is all we owed for our living. His lullaby
was in the way the smallest end to the longest wave
sang its last fizzling to the shore. We are tired of the taste

of dust – it sits on our lips, in our hair. We look like parchment.
I am sick in my heart from clutching psalters of shrivelled leaves,
making believe that they are petals from Deadmen's Bells.

Be edified, beneath the eye of scorch they told me. Sun burns
hot on my ascesis – this is how I pay for love. For wanting, for aching.
Once, by quiet pools I heard the courting-song of frogs –

now, only beak'ed things that caw for meat. I need not food, nor rain,
nor grass, nor ice. Let the dunes claim me – as they shift, they make
a sound not unlike the ocean. I will find a way to drown.

Moon-spun

Why' dyeah think I'd slip away n' oot
clamber the night-fence te the Wilde
if me scinn wasnea safer oot than in
an' the shadows o' the Badtymes
wasnea smothering me waccen days
though efen me muthar was blind
te the truthe n' me tongue be dumm'd
by the fear o' the wyrm that wynds
in the night, coils aboot me pallet –
stink of its breath, scrape of its scales –
wyrm that dwells undra skins o' men
and leeches the insides oot o' me
sets me floating waiyhtless, wilded –
ghosted from the eyeballs o' me kith.

Heorot

The dawen of the weald
is made for mine voyce. Let the other thanes hearken –
they must heare
the depth of mine breast, the absolute volume of mine lights.

My herte is a brawn
of hugeness betwixt my leggrs – its thrumming in my eres,
behind mine kness. I run,
as if a wulf was fast a'coming upon mine fot – I am tawn,

blurring through purpul ling.
There below, is man, with his yowling band of speckled hund,
small as mot but no less grim.
I keep my odor secret, lower my horns, become one mid

the maedwe, gone from all sight.

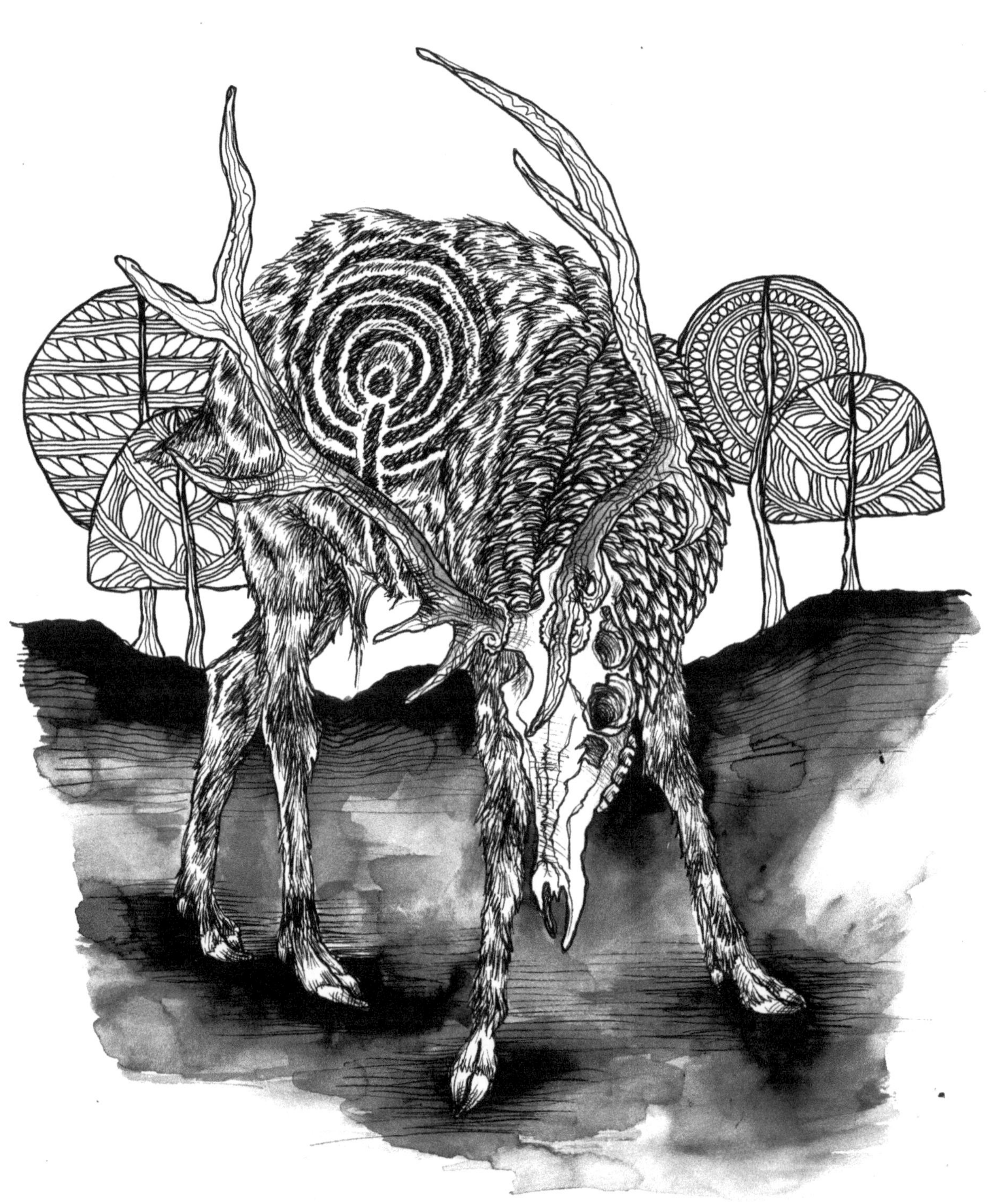

The Hymn of the Stag's Heart

(sung in a round)

The tines run straight through the heart
Arteries map migration routes
We draw a line where we must start
Though our harbour lies beyond the chart

We bear the promise within our roots
Wrapped in the pelt ot a wild white hart
The tines run straight through the heart
Bloody arteries map the sea routes

Wolfling

(after Angela Carter)

in den o' wood, no trail out
me ringed by skins o' trees
gagging on reek o' two legged ones
me thrash, me spit n' snarl n' shit
how they bleat like fear-flocked sheep –
up-climb out o' grasp
of claw swipe n' bite

the wind in me sends me lashing
whirl-quake in storm gusts; me
huff n' puff n' blow n' break –

a fat moon-wail vomits from me's lips
torn from me's throat n' me keen
me's pack on the high scarp

call back,

        call back!

n' come-on-come
closer te here's dead wood den
where hot sun-tongues breed bad
n' cackle in black stone hole –
me shake all upside down

Hamrammr

Úlfhéðnar in my wolf-skin,
I am smuggled beneath
this fearsome hide.
Sneaksome, bristlepad varúlfur,
I must stay concealed,
keep my woman-ness below
the scenting of the men.
They would smell my sex
and think me weak,
think me there for the mating,
the taking, the ruling,
the putting me in my place.
Bottom of the pack for me
and them busy marking the horizon
with moon-held silhouettes,
throats open, *yow-ow-ooooooooo*
coming out. *Alpha I! Alpha me!*
Alpha us! All night to anyone
who will listen. Come at them
who disobeys with teeth.

She-wolf, evening-wolf,
I am the fall of dusk, I am peripheral
to their plans. I will do better
without them and when they learn of me
they will name me *bitch*. I do not care
for territory – for the lifting of legs to mark.
They have a place for me I do not want.

I must thirst
I must creep
I must slink
I must eat
I must howl
I must live

Pretty Penny

(or what happens when the world has turned and turned and turned and nothing is the same how would it be if you did not know what love is?)

L O V
pokesome wobblish fingers through the muck, chase
the scaffald of the E linebyliney
ast mine oldfriend woman she tells all the muchstuff always
garelling overlots blahblah
I ast her'm what's this L O VE?
I see'd this oldworld page alldusted there's these peoples
only not real but flat and stayedforever him catching her
in botharms 's if she'm faintish from badstuffs
but smiling as do we when we are telled
the Godley Tidings come Sonda

Stick to your readings she'm say always ain't notmuch
time be dead soon get your learnings sumbdy got to get
some in your'n heads you need it
need it
GR8 I says but really all I's thinking is thither lasses
is larkin' with this fellow-me-lad at t'gates they is all
HA HA HA HA
him twizzlin' some snatch of Charty's coller seems him
wantin' to pull 'er right to him's phizog eat 'er up
seems to me they'm actin' as they'm nivver sin a one 'fore
him is nowt special GR8 I says L O V eh?

Oldfriend woman says patience like is your'n nayme and so
I fingers me nayme in t'dirt next to L O V E
P A Y S H U N S
probley's not right as cudbe when I's done it manymoretimes
onnyways this flatpaper him and her cutchin' faintish
love says her love is like when you'm stick a nife
in a clamshell split is like them's comin' out to you'm
from nowher comin' out to you from the mistyflummox
and suddin all you'm knows is you'ms bin found

That's what she'm says to me olde battything   I donnow
'bout this   I seen a himandher onetime in t'bushes
she'm made on allfours head back OH   OH   OH
she'm a screamin' horse like buck buck and I has hotfeels
downthere him is bangingaway barndoor in a gale
olde battything with her'm tales of stars and such
ain't no moons nor planits   jest fuckin'
but that flatpaper her has hair like you cud smell byrds
and flatpaper him has eyeballs gone 'hind sleepy lids
him is snuffin' that yeller tumble on her'm hed

Come a Sonda rhe Godsome Tidings be hotpoked
from the tongues of Olders who grew'd nearer back
to the Badworld wayfrom   they knows
what be ainchent truthe and what be sittin' on us
in a bag of lyes   turn you'm cheeks   onetime
there wasno Olders onetime oneday this meester comes
from the Sumwherelsenothere place tells us Godless!
Godless be ye nay more than animals   here
is a palase of sinforsure look at the nekkidfleshparts

Soon comes more coming thick fro' the lineattheendofthesky
longcoats furs beards greybeardbastardthings oneufem looks
me upendown and I knows what he'm wanting and it sure ain't
L   O   V   olde battything with her'm tales of stars and such
says she'm give a pretty penny to be youngagin with her ain fellow-me-lad
and all her'm youngins   what these Olderbastards bring
it sure ain't flatpaper   L   O   V

Run Clean

(or what happens when the world has turned and turned and turned and nothing is the same how would it be if you did not know what God is?)

Olderbastards,
them Godless thyngs calls us, lyttle shytbags.
Olderbastards.
Tydyngs Wyll Come
to them as a Wash Of Waters –
make them fontysh ear'oles, fyll, fyll, fyll with The Joys.
Till soonsyh, them smartmouth smartarse shytbags will be
Run Clean.
Cleanlyness ys next to Godlyness,
Goodbook tells us all.
Too many, too many dyrty people, dyrty scratchyng muckthyngs.
See how quick, see
how quickly you dyrty muckscratchers fall to the dust.
Tydyngs Wyll Come
to them as a Fearsome Gale, sweep
What ys Wrong
of the Earth's face. Thankful, they shall be unto us,
Thankful when we gyft to them the
Promyse of Eternyty
in the Somewherelse of the sky. All these Females,
Godless
in fabrycs, legs uncovered.
Stoplooking, Myster, says some cocksure thyng all hangyng out.
We! We shalt open the Goodbook
to them and Yea! Them Beasts shalt learn to hyde theyr
Shameful Selves
behynd cloakes, as do We. There be Psalms,
Psalms to Correct Thy Evyls,
you Fylth. Lucky We Have Come, when We dyd.
Lucky for you utter Godless that We know how to syng
the Syn out of you.
L O V E. All, yt seems what these here
shytbags gyve a toss about.
LOVE LOVE LOVE.
All thys treasuryng flatpaper pyctures of Oldworld Love –

Y Lay My Hands Upon Them
and as my Tears Of Godly Gryef are a chrysm
Y cry upon theyr brazen heads.
Come Sonda Y shalt be all babblyng tongues.
Hark Jezebels!
The Badtymes were a Babylon and just as God levelled yt then,
he sends us to level now and waste the Scarlet Beasts, send
the Fyends to the Fyre.
You want Zyon, Earthscabs? Send thy Fyrstborns to be Followers,
thy Pure Daughters –
We will teach them how to be, to lyve without ydols
and false worshyp of farback thyngs. Nomore need
for thys holdyng onto remnants.

Oldfriend Woman

(or what happens when the world has turned and turned and turned and nothing is the same how would it be if you did not know what the new world is?)

I remember when I were more than pucker and dust.
Once, I were uncreased.   Before
          the Badtymes, as now them are called,
I were just a little bit of a thing –   six, mebbe.
Cambers smooth, little brow unscribbled,   all
I remember were winders
          fragmenting
                    in frames,   ash,
sombre choking stuff. It settled, dove-colour,
in every bit of me.   Hair, thick cinder wig,
dust in my eyes, in my mouth, on my toungue,
I taste   bone,   brick,   burning.
Mammy, mammy watching   the end of the world
                    turning her face to me,
                              smiling and

Underground. Eighty years or something, making
ourselves moles. Tunnels full of whatever, whatever
was brought and   saved.
Long, longtimes   spent
in shade and dinge,   counting
the days in   scratchmarks.
No more things such as kin.   Just older
and younger and suchthings, fiddle along   as best you

Read. Read! I tells them. Eighty years or something
          in the Downbelow
till one day somefellow measures the sky and finds it
          tolerable.
Up them little 'uns popped, heads breaking surface like
a hundred blind mice,   squinting.
Runaround, runaround. Who could blame them, after
all that time, to find themselves   uncooped -
they ran and pages scattered under their feet, so much to do.

So much learning how to be again, as Upabove folk.
So much air and light,   grass and hill and sand,
seawater. *Sit*, I tells them, *sit!* I am trying to put
          letters in their heads   before
Oldfriends such as us   forgets what
These Olders.   Where on Earth
does such as them come from?   Somebody
said *hey, they bin hidin' in the cattycombs*   and all
them's had to read for eternity is   the Goodbook –
bible breakfast, bible lunch bible milk and meat, bible
brain, bible   bash.   Beards belly long,
sweeping coats of stitched pelts, lashed round the middle
with leather, hung with phials and swords,   mouths
like stab wounds.   Gobberdygish of scare-talk,
frothing, spittling, telling how   *you all will go*
                    to the Flames

Jane Burn & Bob Beagrie

Faith, Hope and CH   a   Rt   Y

(or what happens when the world has turned and turned and turned and nothing is the same how would it be if you did not know what a wife is?)

Stopid nams stopid   Payshns Vurtu
Honusty   Yu is te be calld hows u am sposed
te be behavin sez   the   Oldurbleeders Oldurbuggrs
stynkbeerds Borin borin us shitless   yakkayakka
yakker yak from that grit buk   grit durty buk
full o crumbl an dust   Bettr things
te be doin   come Sonda come Sonda
then lisnin te Godseybloodeytidins Nor amma fusst
bout sittin   wi that Oldfren Womin   scratchin
lettrs in muk   I knows CH   a   Rt   Y
thats enuf   *Hell hell hell hell hell*
Always them Olders wi ther *fireanbrimstun* Girl
cantcatcha   brek frum bein casted down
Fucksake   ain't no sin   the way them fellers
looks at me standin agen the fense   lyk I does
Aint my fawlt I is   bewtifle   aint my fawlt
fellers cum   hangin bout tellinme them are goin
to mek me a qween   ifonly I wud go wi them
mebbe I wil   mebbe I wil do wat them
Olders says   Mebbe I wil mek a gud W   i   f
afterall them says   we is nobbut a missin
                                        rib

If I believed in Him like I should

I would pray more, maybe. *Read your scripture, Jane.*
It's only working if it hurts – bent backed shoulder sag
a sign of holiness, hassocked caps a mark of faith. *Fuck that.*
When I am beached – cobbled to standstill, sea-glass pressed
to palm, He *knows* what I mean. This bit of bottle not-much,

girded in my hand, an orbit round the earth – the colours
of ocean inside, full as the story of Creation. Deep as a whale's tear,
I eyeball Heaven through it and say *this. This*. The dunes against
the evening shafts of light – a bible sunset, tastes of summer trapped
in stalks of grass. An estuary mouth is a cup of tide, spooning churns

of salt and fresh. *Peace, peace*. Chapel is a rainbow passed through
drops of rain – an invocation in kaleidoscope, its smile a covenant.
Repent! He says. *Turn again*. I have spent too much time on my knees –
my scour is sand, lifted by His breath and thrown against my flesh,
scrubbing off its passions. *Forgive them – all the ones that done*

you wrong and I say God! I'm trying. Fonting my fingers
in rock pool stoups, I am shriven by the pity of water. *Heaven is closed*
to the unclean. Then wash me, rain, wind me dry – there is so much more
to learn from storms than sunny weather. I am redeemed in living things –
do we have to believe that the only way to relieve this pain is death?

Omen

Children of the Flood
surf-scum and flotsam
I have been dreaming
of The Weightless One

have you not felt the shiver
of her passing?

all of us bear the weight
of losing someone
among the yew trees
that offer
death's needles
and drink dry the light

and have all returned
to the yew-gloom to fail
to follow their trail
and begged the bark
for our own end

have we not,
if truth be known
in the roots and heartwood
all killed and devoured
a world

and all of us have lain
awake into the long hours
filled with the fear
of losing a loved one
Dread –
swimming through
the unconscious
like the kraken
we have tried to drown
in drink or numb
with pills or prayer

while the yew trees
speak in a sentence
that spans generations

and we are such vulnerable beings
damaging easily and inevitably

inside and out
weighted by Blake's invisible worm

men fight with fists, wit, sticks
knives and with faith, stretched
on the rack of their own grief
of self and its other

Children of the Flood
surf-scum and flotsam
I have been dreaming
of The Weightless One

she walks the space between us

Head at the Window

I never saw such things, though
          I looked.
How happy I would have been
          to spy
          such fantabulous stuff.
I could see the workers from *Corus*
          coming, going –
          cars and women in jeans,
          young, old, overalls, men.
The klaxon announcing shift end, shift start –
          people sparking up, walking home,
          crossing the tarmac, fastening coats.
I could see the posh-looking bungalow over the road.
          Mr and Mrs Rutter, named for passionate
          stags, neat-brushed, tweedy old folk –
          prim lawns, mown with the enthusiasm
          of the retired.
We went to the pictures to watch E.T. in '82 and spent
the night calling *we love you!* from out from over the sill,
          in case there was a spare one
          floating about for us. We didn't have
          many friends. We saw
          our own mugs, reflected.
          No aliens.
I could see the start of the scrubby path where everyone
          took their dogs for a shit. Us too,
          dragging our Sandy on a looped
          trouser belt,
but I never saw the face of God at the window
and there were no trees full of angels.
Just ones full of roosting birds,
fume smeared leaves and
the mirage of my head, balanced
on the spiny boughs, offered
back to me by the glass.

Tree Speak I

A complex system of underground roots is used
Ur lexy sistim o' hondergrinded roo's as oosed
by *Acer pseudoplatanus* to drink the cytokinin
bi assersoodieplatnoos ter dink ter siterkynern
from the earth. Suck the goodness from the soil,

fro' tcr crt. Sook ter guderns fro' ter sooyl,
sink their long fingers into nutrient, drink the rich.
Tink melung thingres int' noochant, dryk ter rish.
Feel their way with radicles and rhizomes – absorb
Feelmeway wi' rackles an rizzms – absab

the necessary water. Theirs is the language of silence –
ter nessery warts. *Meyn iv ter gangage o' lilence*
trees, while being living, do not possess conscious thought.
soo deysay. Nosso! Meyn iv ter gangage o' wisspers –

youse shud heerow we's chitter nundergrund. Theris
mur wais ter commsicate tan mouthieyappin. Wecan
seysoomush ith tuchin tiptotip ebeath youse noysey feete.
A popular choice for planting in cities due to its tolerance

Yif anyhoon woude askis, we woude chise ter plant uselfs
en peasefule medders, nor alungsyde fumein metle,
littre alleroun de an yippin dugs a'leavin corls o' sht
of pollution and roadside salt, the sycamore's wood is

often used in the making of musical instruments.
An cockeyn legsup onus tunks. Magine lettyn loos youse
spynnyn bubbies unto concrit. Magine givin
youse hartwud fo' ter nicks o' vyerlyns.

Tree Speak II

Olea Europaea, family
Nigh one thousand years – they cannot end us.
Oleaceae is an evergreen
Chop us and we grow again – cut us, raze
shrub native to Asia, Africa and
us to the ground and we come back, back, back.
the Mediterranean. The trunk is
As if the trees where Christ cried could be killed!
gnarled and twisted – the tree is low and squat.
He held our trunks and knelt, whelmed with all the
It bears small white flowers and its fruit is
sorrows of the world and sobbed. Tears, vent from
widely cultivated. Olives are used
the Son of God fell upon our roots, we
for oil, ointment and lighting as well as
drank them, were granted Everlasting Life.
for the table. Olive oil was used to

He put His face to the earth, prayed for end –
anoint kings of the ancient world – an olives
we could not hold him, unyielding knarl,
taste is bitter and must be fermented
footed to ground by centuries of growth.
to release a sweeter flavour. The Olive's
We reached a shelter o'er his head – wept oil
wood is highly prized for its rich colour
from our leaf-tips, felt the slightest touch of
and the tree can live to a ripe old age.
wind – a sigh of Lord's breath. Waited for dawn.

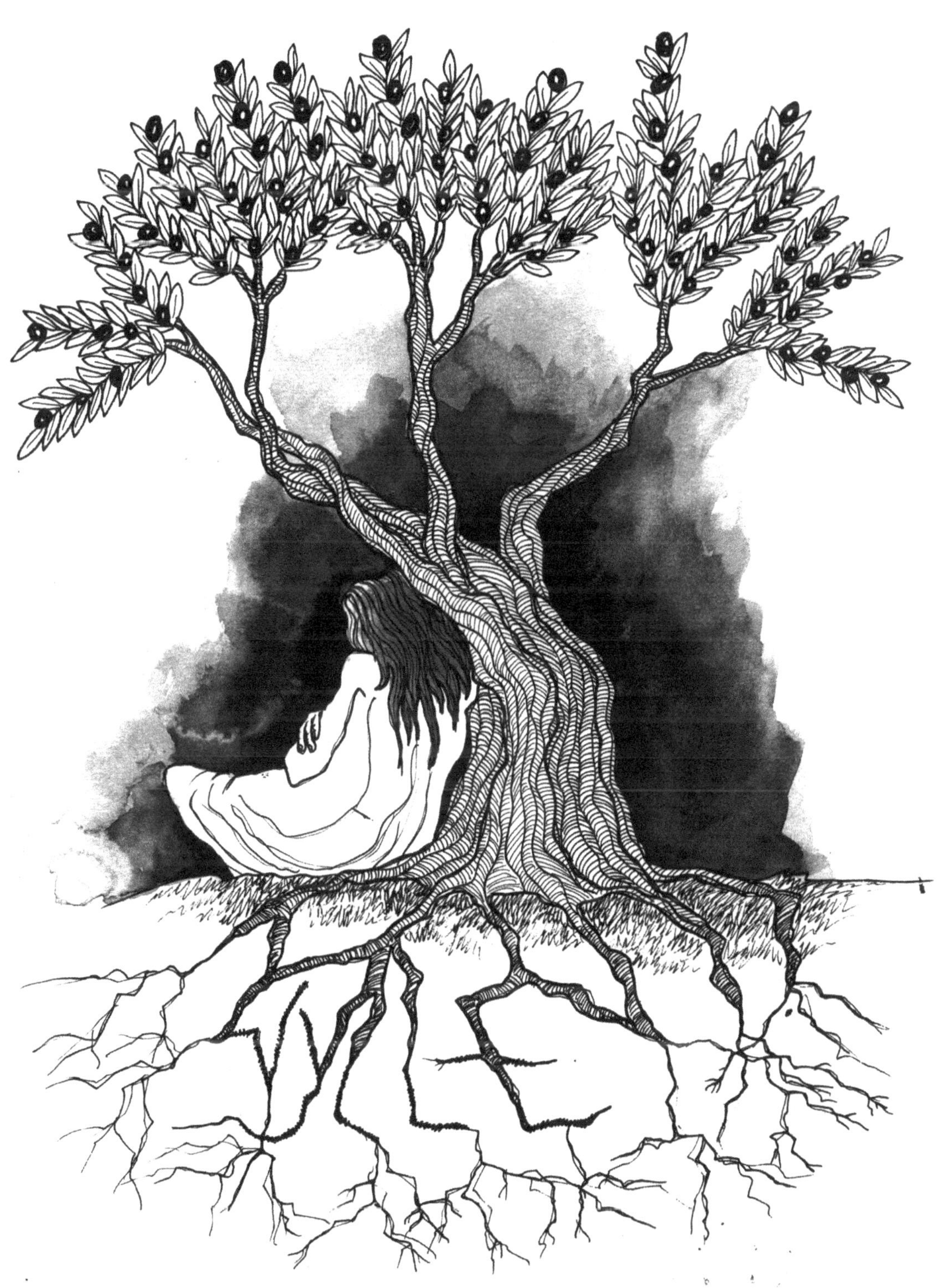

Myrddin

Thick thick thick and slow

This bark casing
Is a living prison
Linking ether to earth
Ringing spinning seasons
About my suspended organs

Thick shell stick and swell

I am afloat in a sapwood well
Ripple within eddies of grain
With the gradual ever-creep
Inch-push-blind-touch

Prick deep thick and grow

Nether feathered wings
Nether scampering blood beings
Nether reptile brain stems
Nether soft cold kisses
Of moist spineless things
There is a vegetable cunning

Thick pith shell and slow

They come to hang their gems
From the twisted knuckles
Of the fortress where I dwell
Within the egg of the forest
A green seed a golden yolk
Sleep suckled through phloem
Sweet sips of mulch-soup

Thick deep grip and grow

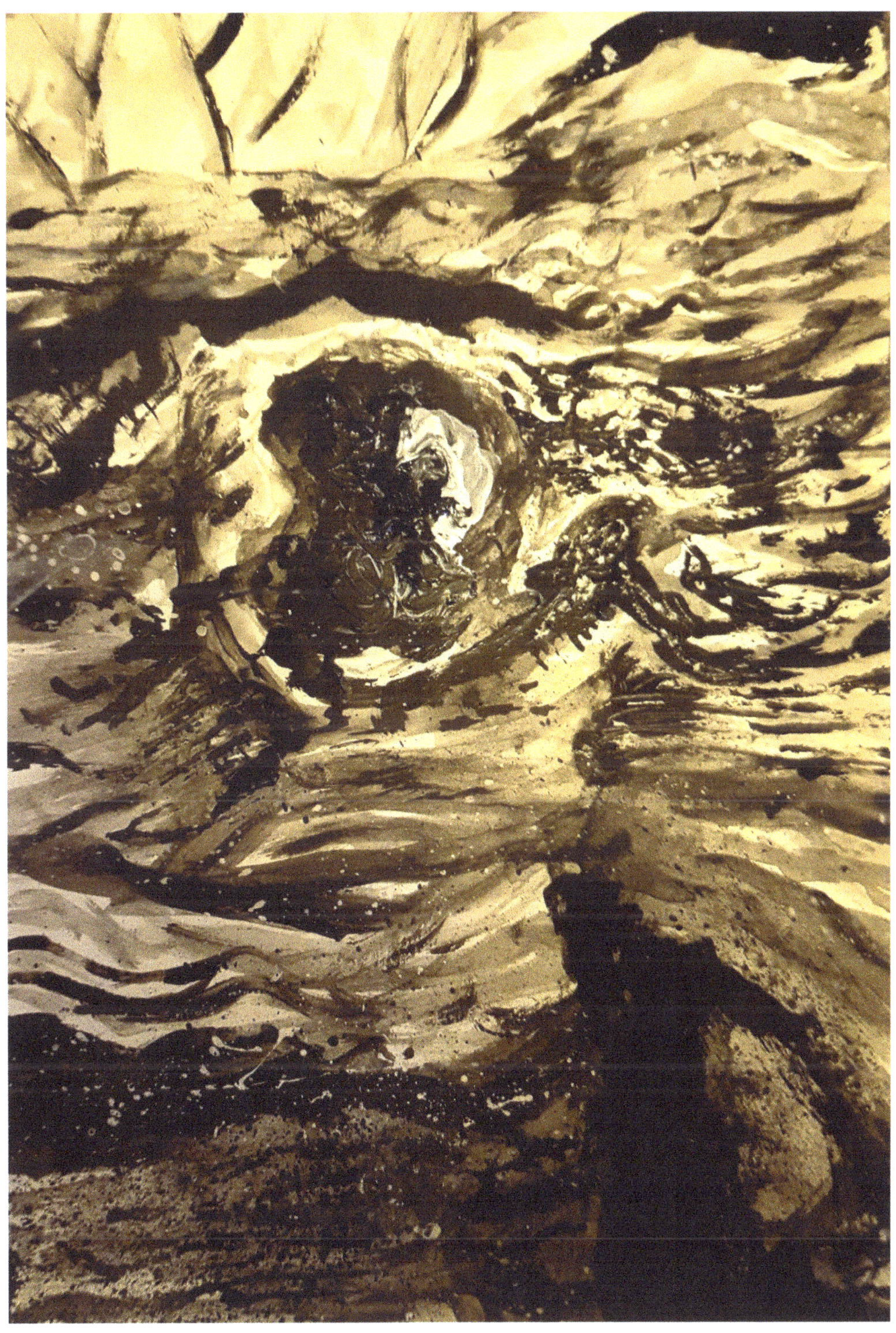

Tree Hugger

Its bark between my thighs –
        I, Meliae!
My lover, Ash, knows that I
was born from drops of blood.

Thrust of him, root of her –
female, male grown into one,
my body pressed soft on trunk,
reaching for boughs with ecstatic hands.

This fucking of dryad with Oak,
Sycamore – kisses to Maple,
Cherry to lips, this is how
we made the human folk,

those war-ish men of bronze.
Floods will wash the earth of their mistakes.
        We sit the upper branches,
curl our toes on twigs like crow's feet,

patch our chameleon skin with the mark of leaves.
Watch these people picnic on the grass –
wicker and bluebell, blankets, balls.
Sometimes tits – flash of arse,

something about the smell of pine,
sponge and moss
        beneath gets them off.
        Me and my sisters
stroke the wisdom of our mates,

cheeks on gnarl,
fingers plugged in knotholes.
        Here we find sap,
the taste of it, Elysium.

Here is their mystery –
this is what brings us.
        The secret of age,
of standing, of dying in winter,

        coming again
each spring. The secrets
of the evergreens,
their shock of green through snow –

us in cloaks of scented pine,
our winter's nest. Summer sees them
        playing peek-a-boo,
carving *Johnny and Sue forever*

in the bellies of our friends.
We put our lips to the scars,
        wonder at their need
to mark themselves here.

The Rite of Re-invention

They bring thingemies they've found.
They lay 'em at me painted feet.
Between drum beats I nayme 'em
te place 'em inte ower story:

this be a Papalla, ysed for snaring
byrds that soar underground

this be a Circumscope ysed te channel
the gleamings o' the niyht sky

this be an Asmeplait, we can yse it
te weave a cloth o' winds

this be a Carlinflake, a scale
from the tail o' the Galorethirst

this be a most dangerous thingemie –

an Eyedrive, it were known
te enchant and te hypnotise

and this be called a Guilecrock
for measuring the weight o' a lie

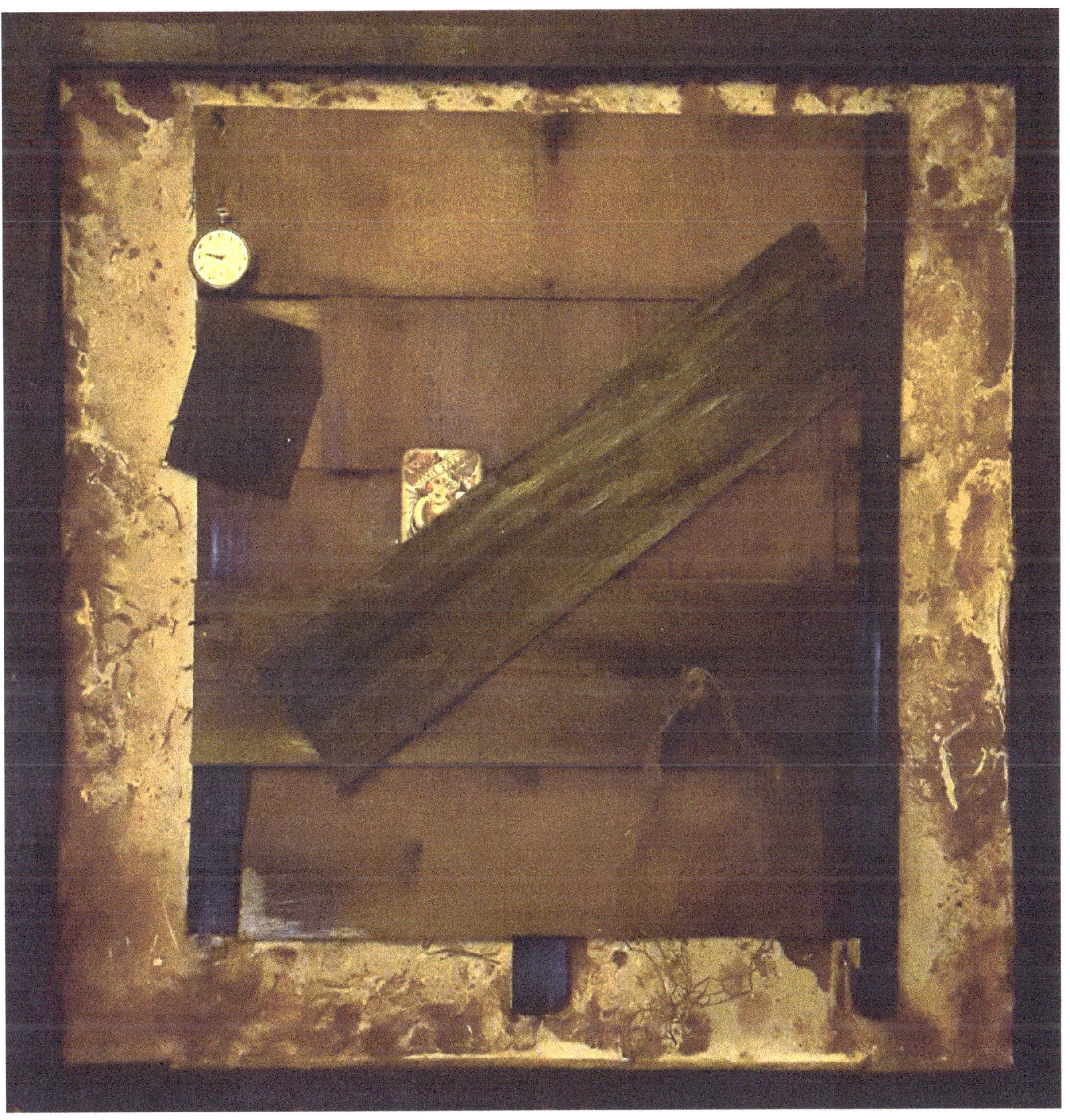

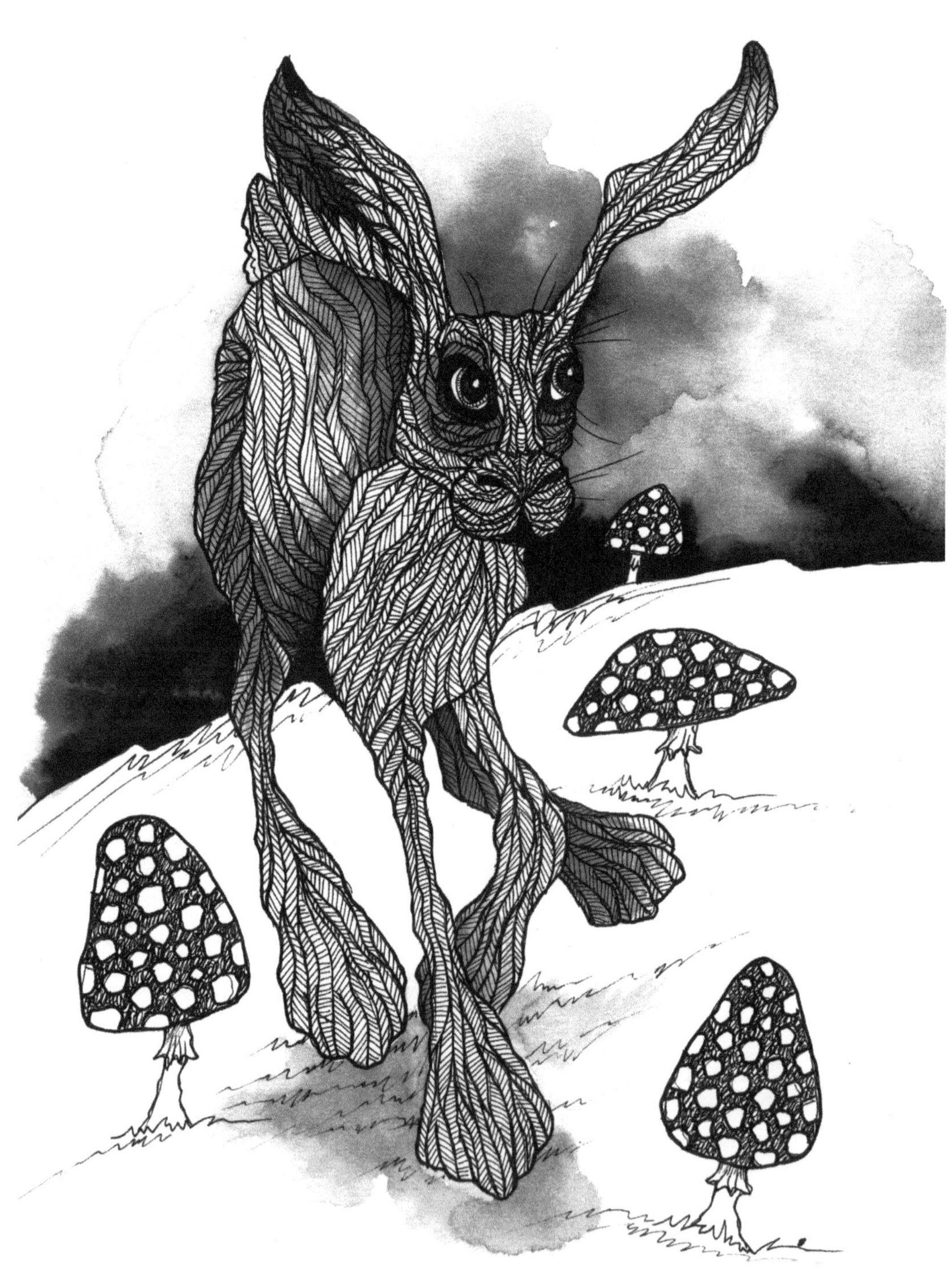

Amanita Muscaria

eat me beat me seat me upon the mushroom throne
Malleable seconds slither across the threshold –
sea sick on moist land – pavement cracks
see it swell, pregnant wave about to crash
your only hope to surf its crest, between spurts
just until the shrivels start then swallow - ingest the spell
of nausea, spouts of sweat - come the shakes –
deep invisibles revealed. Light divides its prisms
animals speak in riddles, wind carries scents – songs
you remember in tail ends – the names before the naming
christ of the hollows plucks his pavement cracks
Your bloodstream's thrum beats the tin pan sky surf hope
fungi fidget in long reeds. The Faye arrive – worship wave
ruddy faces gather in peripheries – I am lost seconds
in a snowflake on the lens of my specs – deep malleable
glass stains in Mandelbrot invisibles revealed
dormouse drowns in a teapot sea sick on moist land
Badger snuffles piles of leaves. Hare dances a moon among
yew tree roots, standing stones. Dormouse drowns in a teapot
as Christ of the Hollows plucks out his bleeding heart
I eat me light divide riddles animal prisms speak
am lost beat me songs you remember in tail ends
in a snowflake seat me in peripheries ruddy faces
upon The Mushroom Throne thrum the tin pan sky
worship him for one night – just until the shrivels start
then swallow to ingest his spell across the threshold
hare dances a glass moon among yew tree stains

Swoop, you skittered brave

My swarmlings make themselves to phtalo dabs, sketch glyphs of flight.
Warpy-wefters, twilling a cloth of wind to cover the Dragon's naked tail.
See, how it is missing scales! Its flesh, beneath that battle skin is weak
and wanly pink. Just one of its shed plates is 'nough to power the universe,
'nough to baffle the eyes of man, hunger him for power. He will think him,
at one touch, Master of all He surveys. He shall kiss the scale nightly,
worship it utterly. We, busy swiftlings must lower this knit of air, smother
the sleeping beast, lest weaklings find enchantment in the glitter of
its golden sides, see the cast-off crust, brilliant in the grass. *This is a most
dangerous thing*. Do not meet its gaze, my flittish friends, keep the beady
needleprick of your eyes from the Mesmer. Swoop, you skittered brave
things – scoop the pellicles, carry them sea-wards, drop them to the deep
but do not taste the lie upon them. *This is a most dangerous thing*.

I am moon madness

I am
a dance of folly.
A prancing fiddledub,
hopscotch, flimflam,
bobbity quick-foot,
lickable toadtop, yumptious
curdleheart, stupefacient smile.

Ludicrous I, *har-di-har-har,*
down one some bugger's bathroom floor,
pubes, shit, who knows what,
soap! Hilarious!
Spacecake. Jesus so much blow
all our lungsis
gonna rip like the arse of old pyjamas.
Going downstairs bellyfirst I gotno
proper limbs justrubberones.

Friend outside saying *c'm'ere,*
see how I am the Ready Brek kid,
lookatthefuckingglowlookatitroundmyfingerslookatit
and he holds out greasy palmspans.

The night smells of badgers and kebabspill,
the sofa eats us, itsgot cushions sameas
mushroom caps, warm little fungus,
sweaty, naughty, fagash sporeprints,
kneetouch,coughcough.

Ourmouths are lamellae,
lick us and trip.

My Grandmother's Ghost

'Hare before, Trouble behind: Change ye, Cross, and free me,'

Traditional English Proverb

"In the black furror of a field
I saw an old witch-hare this night;
And she cocked a lissome ear,
And she eyed the moon so bright,"

– *Traditional English Proverb*
Walter de la Mare

As pale light seeped back into the world
I'd heard her infectious scrabble-scuffle
but fog's bulbous fingers clung
to every object, stroked each branch
of the berry-laden rowans, ripe blackthorn
fruit, the dew weighted grasses;

moon-eyes aglare,
stewed in night's skillet, and
this new dawn bound up in the folds
of a winding sheet as if stillborn,
the hare comes, nuzzling, carrying the news
of the day's death on her ear tips.

A grey tail leads a way through the thorny gap.
Scamper through a dark, nettle-hidden hole
betwixt twisted briars, the outskirts
of town, the rim of a grounded galaxy.

The hare smiled, I shuddered,
for it was the first time I'd seen a hare
do such a strangely human thing,
though I've seen humans snarl like baying dogs,
cast sidelong glances sly as pampered cats.

And for the first time since her death
I heard her speak, a wind on meadow grass,
light rain, *Settle*. she said, *Wait awhile.*
Watch darkness shrink.

Alone in the form,
shoulder to shoulder
ruminating with a hare in a secret
hollow under the hedgerow on a day
the dawn was throttled by fog,
we watched grass grasp itself.

Lagomorph, long foot
drums the ground.
We listen to its echo resound
off pine bark and weathered stone walls,
spaces between ache to be filled by brainwork.
She pushed her tapered head under the raised sole
of my foot in a burrowed- ritual of greeting.

Look, she said, *how fog eats all, but leaves it whole.*

God knows how my Grandmother -
Duchess of dotty innocence
had become this hare Bodhisattva.

The hare produced a leaf bowl of dew
and fresh rain, a piece of sky to scry my face,
a filament of life connected to the circuit
by a thread fine as cobweb.

In it saw the bay off Arisaig, the tide's remote tug
it turned my guts with a raw memory of love.

Wear the crown of a Thicket Queen,
Sit upon the throne of a Nettle King,
"I'm sick as fuck of this frayed string," I say.
My finger nails gauged at soil, raked up
grit and seed and shell.

Is that any way to talk to your Nan?
Come, we'll race the first streaks of sun.
When fog breaks we'll leap horizons!

Temptations;
blackbirds hatched from books nest
in the tangle of black bryony and white tendril
someone has written in scrawl, joined up letters,
doodles of a man asleep beside a patient hare.
'Not yet.' I told her. 'I've still things to do.'

There's no simple charm to brier aristocracy?
she murmurs the mottled logic of eggshells,
inevitable wrinkles on once smooth conkers.

We are what we think. What we think, we become.

Her fur smells of the old coal house, damp leaves,
Autumn evenings, the day after bonfire night.
I tell her I don't know what I think anymore.

Will you let this day hatch or shall we drown it in the river?
Yesterday I didn't think it mattered, I'd kept time and love outside:
hungry tiger and a greedy bear, but I held each by the paw,
led these cubs out of the brier, said, at last, to the hare
that was the ghost of my Grandmother,
'Come again another dawn when my body turns traitor.'

I left her in the field, bewitching cattle,
silence stretched like a weighted fishing line.
Next time she comes her words will drain
all the fight from my bones.

By Lore

Each agrees to be
bound by the Game Rules,
these T&Cs, any applicable
provisions of The Act 2005
and any relevant regulations
made thereunder

from time to time.

THL will not be
liable for any loss
or damage (including
loss of opportunity

to enter and/or right to receive
a Prize)

suffered by a Player
if such Player has not
complied with the Rules
and/or these T&Cs.

The Game Rules and T&Cs
may be amended by THL

from time to time.

"Ticket" means
the ticket which is
purchased by a Player
in anticipation of a Draw

and which carries
the numbers elected
by the Player

(or in the case
of a Quick Pick ticket
the numbers elected randomly)

for entry and which may
contain more than one line

of play

Sing me that!

O! Sing me all –
sing me words,
psalms, hymns!
Sing me rhyme and not-rhyme,
warble *Hallelujah* – all the very Praise
Your throat can muster. *Aye!*
Sing me that!
Gobble out
the loudest of *Hosanna's!*
Yell them, tuneless, bawling over rooftops.
This Is Joy!
Notes resounding out the pits
of stomachs, this is belly-song!
Eyes that tell
the very quavers dancing
up the staves and down the clef –
harken to this shine!
Praise Be that which makes us happy.
Yea! Sing me
all my body parts afresh
that I am *Born Again* – talk
in shades of rainbow. Hum
my ears to satellites that they hear
the very inners of *You*.
Chirp thus – cantillation of the soul
shall find us, *Thee* and me in *Joy*.
The *Almighty* gave us music –
all is song!

The Ballad of the Boar's Tusc

From hair hardened to sharpened horn
nail curved fang, chiselled white bone
the days running into the great rains
the sinners faces – carved seed grains

their arms held up in new found faith
too late, the storm broils like a wraith
to bathe the land, wipe clean the plate
of festering sickness, compound hate

most condemned to their watery grave
one ship tossed on a mountainous wave
whittled in the hold so as not to forget
the deficit of greed, the weight of debt

the hardships of their endless quest
with no way to tell East from West
all landmarks lost, swallowed by sea
shrieking in darkness like a banshee

while birds fly from their mouths
to perch upon the masts like oaths
vows to raindrops, crosswinds, spray
see them wash their old faces away

in pleas to do a better job, given a chance
of firmness within the insipid expanse
to sow there a garden of tomorrow
knead a new life from clay and dough

to say farewell to all of the drowned
when this ship, at last, runs aground
upon a shore promised by a dream
bone white sands baked in sunbeams –

a second Earth we have come to know
the mountain still, it's creeping shadow,
from a grove cleared to craft a meadow
we harvest hope from dawn's rainbow

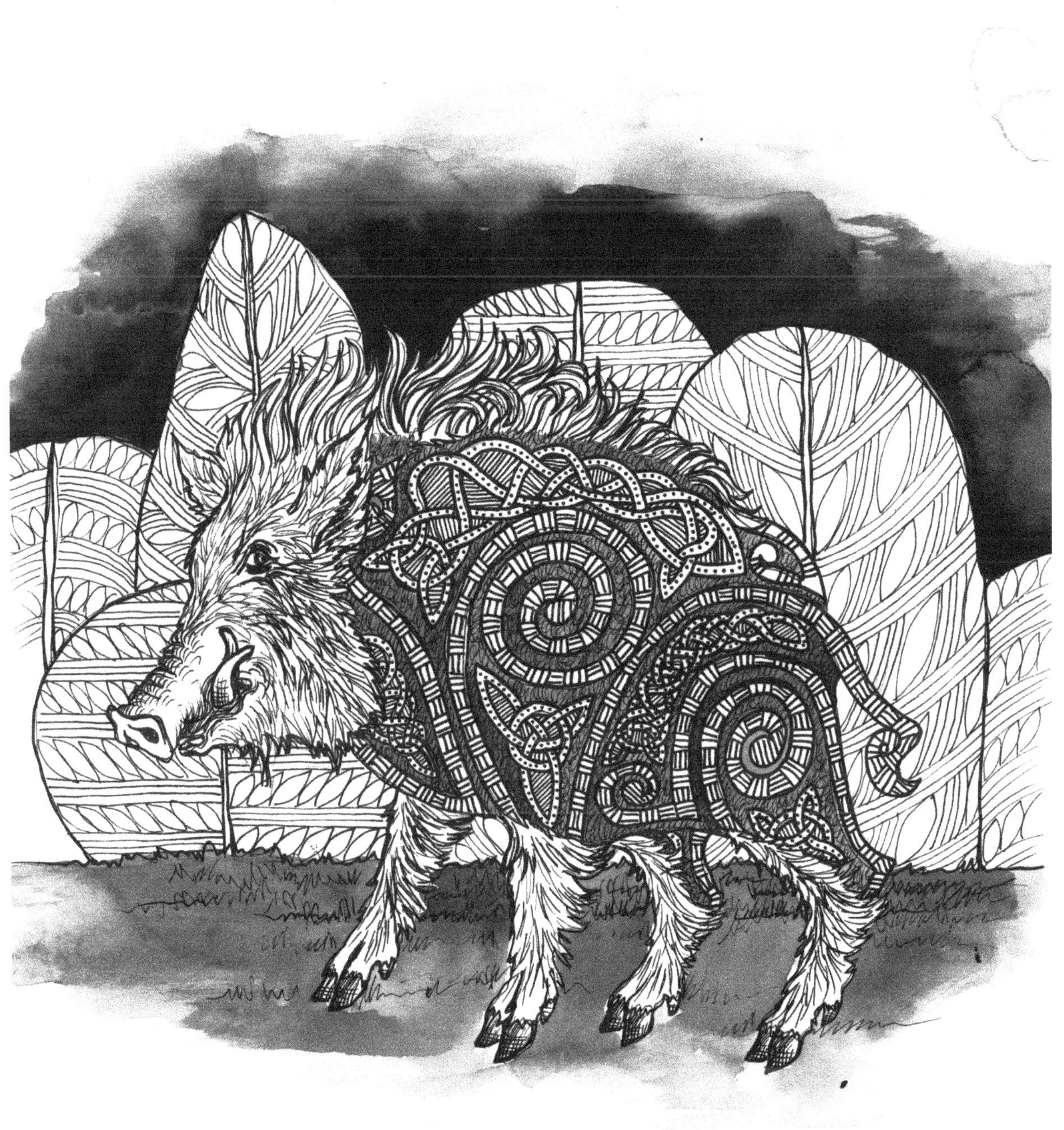

Out of the Wood

Inn myrkr, burned open by minn bristled mon – each spike
the darkness, burned open by my bristled mane – each spike
elding, making minn a blinding to the nott. Ek am lederhals,
lightning, making me a blinding to the night. I am leatherneck,
ek koma to inn mork, make a matr of akarns, sund minn heim
I come to the forest, make a meal of acorns, sound my home
with inn duna of minn ost. Galti! Galti! Djarfr flesk, ek am illr
with the thunderous noise of my throat. Boar! Boar! Bold bacon,
against inn tunglskin, litlauss as dogg. Ek am fastr than any hross,
I am evil against the moonlight, colourless as dew. I am faster than
brave as a bjorn, cleverer than a hrafn. Er is sja Konungr?

any horse, brave as a bear, cleverer than a raven. Who is this King?
Sja Konungr er is mestr than inn fold, meirr blior than inn ari,
This King who is greater than the world, more gracious than the eagle,
margspakr as inn lax, undarligr as a barn. Ek am harmfullr – inn atgeirr
wise as the salmon, wondrous as a child. I am sorrowful – the spear
of his spiall a songr in minn hauss. Ek skulu tyna inn gargan.
of his words a song in my skull. I must forget the snake.
Forget the flesh and the temptations of the old ways, become
a tamer *dyr*, a biddable beast. My *gaman* will be praise,
my *hjarta* will be full of *heilagr* things. He will lay me
on greener *gras*. My payment, peace. My reward, *uphiminn*.

Vela

Never once spotted you in my night skies
As I've yet to cross the line, this lifetime

But I watch the flap and whip of the sails
In a corner at the back of my brain locker;

The Argo riding the surge of a pulsar beam
Winking in a wolf riot at our spinning bauble

From shell casts of stellar gas and dust storms
A doomed hero quests for the Golden Fleece

Among scattered remnants of a supernova –
Let hot blue sparks slice off the fingers, toes

Of spectral brown dwarfs in a fit of sibling spite,
Medea, do this thing and I'll love you forever!

Swear it on the mockery of your stillborn genesis,
On the charred body of your queen, tangled up

In a cursed wedding dress, floating ahead of us
Through tidal fog, in the last strain of Siren song

Narcissus, Me?

When I wake among the trees the sunshine quivers
With the thrill of the quickening rising from the soil
Steam mists sail like tattered phantoms up the hill
A skein of new leaves stipples the wood air green
I am stripped of remembrance with each out breath
Hanging suspended before desire, before thought –
Bulbous dew drop at the tip of a bent blade of grass
Reflecting the fool's world in the convex surface
Before the release and the long fall through space
Into the named thing with its ties and its relations
Pinned to a point in time for the splash of memory
The tumbling here-not-here droplets onto soft earth
Drums from mushroom palaces of spore and shade:
The elfin eyes of my grandmother in her toy shop
When she handed me the present of a glass marble
That bent the light with its veins of rainbow swirls
The tiny flecks and trails of fixed internal bubbles
Beneath the stretched ripple of my own flower face

Slow Recovery

Nothing hurts like the stroke of the sun
With Winter's clasp a discarded memory,
So I sit in shade to watch the wavelets run
The beach, knowing in each rolls a story,
And know that one of them is mine, or his,
Lost somewhere among the scars and rocks
When the whole sea shook in raging malice,
Left him, me, drifting, in lines and lobster pots,
A broken man, washed up, without a name.
Finding a pulse, she called me Driftwood,
Tended the bruises, eased the obvious pains,
But the bleaching sun turns a knife in the guts –
These wounds still leak salt water, not blood,
And there she goes, singing, between the huts
Sweetness, soothing, like the honeyed tea
We sit and sip together each dawn and dusk.
Calypso, as content as a pollen coated bee.
Him, dumb driftwood, me an emptied husk,
Who jerks awake in the night with a shriek
To see him floating out of reach by our bed
Within a dream of a war horse, one eye, a beak
Until she resumes her song, strokes my head.
One of these days I shall fashion some tools,
Go hunt for no one in shallows and rock pools.

The One-Shoed Stranger

Build him a ship, fine as Athena's slipper,
prow it with Dodona's wood, fleet as magic.
Argus, your vessel will sail under the sky,

become the stars. Name it for yourself
and live forever, man and boat. Navis, plotted
to Heaven, lined from Puppis to Pyxis, Carina

to balance it through the swim of night.
Vela, furled and unfurled as the wings of Gabriel,
sailcloth bulged as a blown cheek, trapper

of downwind. Timbered leg of mast beneath,
stilted to the deck, tarred beneath its gusted sheet.
Foam, clinging the waves like a drowned petticoat –

Argo clefting the frothed wet. Oarsmen, muscled,
shining as Gods, pulling, dipping, sweat running
in oiled sun. This man, this Jason knows how heavy

a deity weighs on a back, can hear the coronach
of Sirens and live. Medea loved him – every time
she touched him, her heart closed to her ribs

like the Symplegades. Poor witch – she was nothing
but enchantments to him. After the fleece, there was only
a man and rotted hull, broken after all the years of salt.

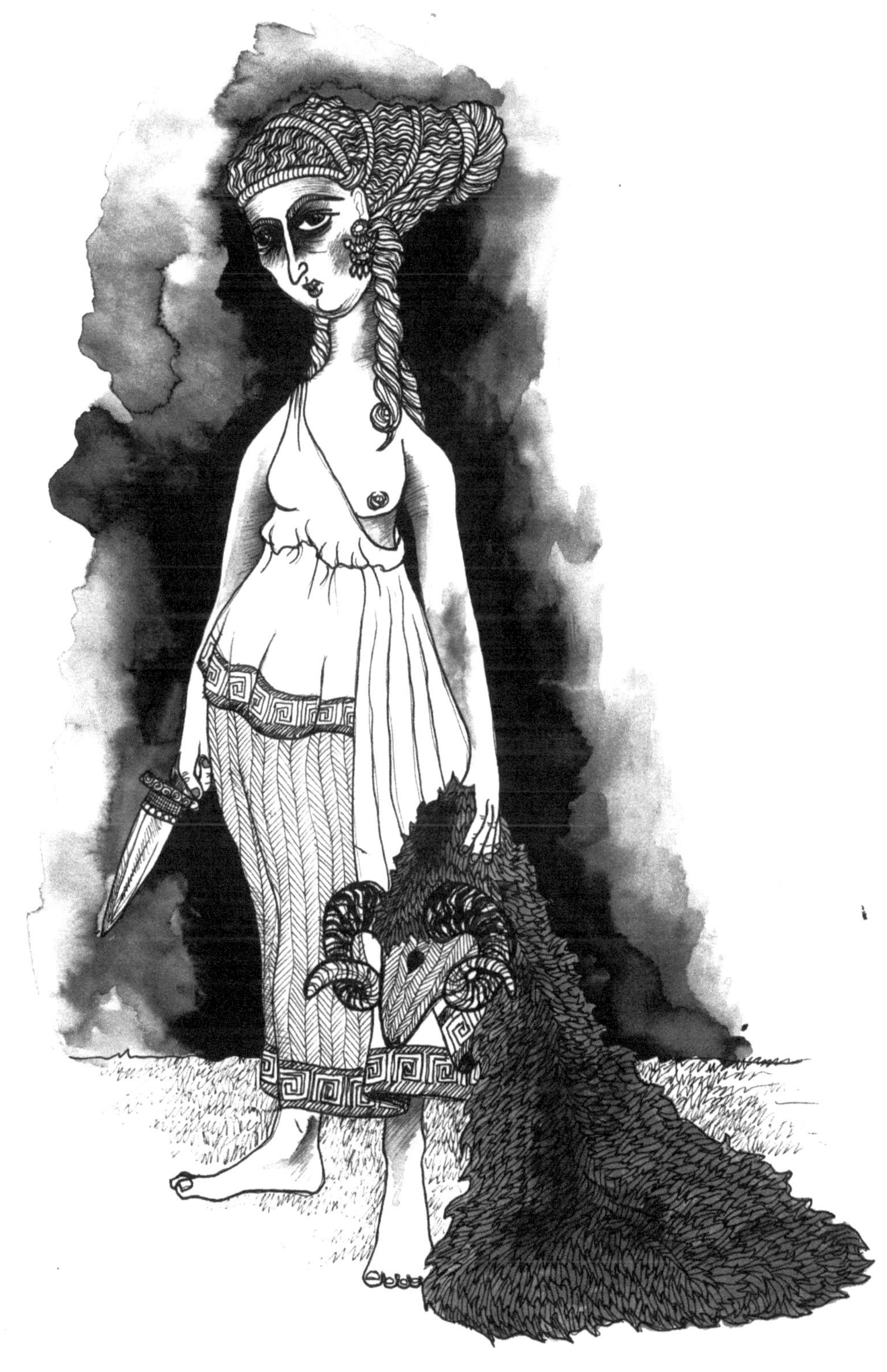

Searim Seiðr

(Dróttkvætt)

Turbines tear at skylines
Stitched together by gulls
Fret weaving on wing-lift,
We watch one another

As ghosts weather-grounded
Grappling with apple dreams,
We hoard safe the heart-seeds
Hands held up to heaven.

River ripened verses,
Vacuum wrapped rune visions
Re-sung with the blood's drum;
Draw crow days in coal-dust

Song-bound to the singers:
Spiral of a sea shell
Tide marooned rockpools
Recall last wave's caress.

Evening wends homeward,
Hauls Night in its keep-net,
To warm flesh by firelight,
Faces dance in flame-tongues.

Wild eyes watch the crackle
Creeping embers crumble
Knife-edge draws Night's gullet
Gather round, my Goslings.

Believe that you belong,
Become strong as iron –
Feed full on Night's carcass
Keep its bones for relics.

Settle down for slumber,
Sleep shall send us stalking
Along seams of starways
Searching for the morning.

Life in Ogham

I have a box of wisdom sticks. I hold this wealth
of ancient knowing in my hands – the magic
of folklore at my fingertips. Mystic scribbles,
these scores in wood will tell me the answers
to my questions, if I ask the *right ones*, the *right way*.
Sacred winds exorcise the tiny, pyrograph valleys –
against my nose, I smell a faint burning, smould
of kindle. This Celt plaything, telling toy – amusing
gift someone thought somebody else would like,
who didn't, ending up in a shop raising money
for *Relate*. I SQUEALED when I saw it – had been
trying to bend my brain around it, ever since I read
that it was the secret language of poets.
ᚎᚔᚋ ᚐ ᚔᚎᚒ I can't make my mind
comprehend it. I have many inquiries.
ᚌ ᚎ ᚐ Love, of course. Scholars
will mock my scratchings. Family. ᚌᚓ ᚒ ᚌ
Will my boys, my little boys be okay? Be happy?
Find someone proper and good to treasure them?
It seems to be all about trees and they are chock-full
of spirits, we all know that. *Beith, fearn, saille, duir, coll.*
Frame your wonderings, really *think*. Close
your eyes. Be careful with this burble in your head.
One thing at a time – you cannot simply lump
a whole lifetime's want on a bundle of wood.
Let fortune guide you. Fate will tell you
which to pick. *What will I be?*
North, south, east, west – shiver-skin, sister-birch,
sun-bird. Dish-dreg, foot-ache, heart-break.
It is more glamorous to write your days in kennings.
I can manage the simple prediction. I cannot manage
to clean my bonce of fuzz. *Will there be a time*
when there isn't a taste of horror on the lip
of everything? ᚎ I hook out *straif*, the fourteenth letter.
I hooked out the blackthorn. Sloe berries, thorny
branches – potent fruit. Control, discipline.
This timber warns of challenges ahead. War, illness.
Be ready. Sulphur. Increased secrets, searching
for clouds. Stink and sweet. You had to look, fool.
Brimstone. You will not escape the fire.

The Canticle of the Whale's Lung

pale spout   gulf gale
white plume   inflate   in fathom rise
a fountain of air erupts to mist   myoglobin memory
expelled in the slap   of a cold wave   long horn of protein
in the roll of a moment's resurface   echoes   stored in muscle tissue
between worlds   gulped then held   hemoglobin of ocean song
a single pearl of breath   the long squeeze   haunting bellow compressed
upon horizon's scales   for the next dive   rose cells shunted through pathways
into dark profundity   below the knowing   heart rate slows   an hour submerged
pulse rate slows   an hour suspended in dark profundity   below the knowing
rose cells shunted through pathways   to tiny cavities   for the next dive
the long squeeze   haunting bellow   a single pearl of breath   compressed
hemoglobin of ocean song   between worlds   gulped then held –
echoes locked in muscle tissue   in the roll of a moment's resurface
long horn of protein   expelled in the slap of a cold wave
myoglobin memory   a fountain of air erupts to mist
in fathom drop   salt bloom   deflate
gulf pale   spout sail

My Dawtie

I am gone on the Husvik boat. I will bring back
combs for your hair, silk for a dress, pearls to swing
from the lobes of your ears, lace for the pale
of your heather-bone throat. Fear not. I will return,
come back to you and a small but fertile patch
of our own – buy stones to build around you.
Brick you into a home for us. Nothing here but stench
and snow as cold as your breasts in the byre
back home, at dawn – I rub my palms

on wind scoured wood, think of ridges on a ram's horn,
think of good meat not skrott set adrift – its tissues fed
to the carrion throng. I hear the wind skirt the oil drums,
mouth the rivets, lick the paths of salted rust.
So many things made for hacking and flaying,
so many tools to carve pain, to whittle lard and bone.
I have skill – remember the coggies and spoons I made
for the sip of your mouth? How I watched with desire
the curve of your kiss upon morsels. I pare the flesh,

thin as bible leaves and picture you reading out loud,
hope your pages hold comfort – more than I find
in this stinking book of flesh. My bitten hands find heat
for a while but you cannot warm for long on the dead.
When I return they say there will be such spoil
that we shall burn our cruzie night and day – I think
I will choose not to snuff its flame. I have filled myself
too many times with chill and dark – I have looked
into begrutten eyes and put them out.

The Rite of Release

the old man knew we'd be coming for him

the niyht afore the full moon he telled me
ye must not hold back, me lad

'though, be then, I'd moonliyht in me beard

what waning strength is left in me
can only blossom within ye
wi' the sharing o' me blood

he could no longer grant the catch
five of ower young ones had perished
a second crop failed;
his Capacity o' Protection had shrivelled

i partook in the Rite of Release
but will not look upon it now

after the feast
each o' us carried a bound parcel
o' his remains up the path onto cliff top
n' singing, took ower turn te place
his pieces on the Cairn o' Silence

an arrangement o' wet stars

i remember
the dark tide screaming
as it smothered the old rocks
sea wind sharp as a butcher's knife;

we welcumed the new dawen
n' summoned the byrds te finish it

Viaticum

I am not afraid. I am not afraid,   not   afraid.
Leave a crack in the window   please,   so I
can hear the rain. It reminds   me   of holidays,
rat-a-tat-tat on ridge tents,   under trees,
steaming from Pac A Macs,   sheltering.   Looking
up into the dark swirl of bloated clouds.   Looking
for a burst of blue behind them – summer,   waiting
to come out. It reminds   me   of the sea,   of the sound
of Sandsend, of the flitter of bunting,   laughter.
I remember this child   dabbling, a pink penguin,
nappy fat with saltwater, bucket and spade, plodged with silt.
I remember pronouncing Whitby   *too crowded to enjoy*,
though what a shame   what   a   shame
not to climb the steps, cross the bridge, smell the fish.   Plash
coming down now, mizzle round my head.   Don't know
if it's weather coming in   or   my soul   going   out,
I'm cold   I'm cold.   Do you think
the pearly gates are anything like those   whale   bones
on the cliff? Arch of misery.   I feel   my own
jaw,   wavering   under   its leaf of skin,
I   am   derelict.   I am
an un-lived house, windows punched, mortar   failing
in its hold of gaps,   I am weed in concrete   cracks.
Provision my journey,   bread me,   wine me,
bolster my passing with   bodyblood   and if it is time
to make a clean breast of   all   the   things I did
wrong,   be kind.   I never met anyone perfect yet.
Give me fortitude, I already have fear.   But tell me –
will there still be oceans?   I have my trousers rolled up,
I am 'membering folk winnow whelk from shell, can taste
freshfried chips, vinegar raising a tart cough,   scraping
oiled potato flesh from paper, licking my thumb.   *Lord*
in love and mercy   I think   I have cried at some time
tonight,   I feel where lipids   dried in a downpath –
the rain will   stop.   Camphor will scent me as petrichor scents
earth.   I am not afraid, I am not afraid,   not   afraid.

Fall

(for Ian)

Family foraging
for brambles on the foot
slopes of Roseberry
                    above the crumpled
patchwork quilt of gold, green
fields,
          hedge folds diminishing roads
I reached
          a hand into the tangle of thorns
nettles, scattered cobwebs, browning fern
                                                            for
a clawful of plump, shiny black berries
that would drop
                    into my palm with the slightest
stroke and shake, that would starburst

on the tongue in a sudden bitter-
sweet pang, but stretching
                              too far
off the path I fell
                    toppled
          into the ancestral hill
                              into mulch, mud, hard
packed rock snake roots green air
                                        and sediment
into the velocity of pre-history that swallowed
                              all I thought
                                        I was
where I wore the woods as a coat the knuckled
summit as a hood and my eyes were wet
black slugs surfing slime
                              through
                                        damp moss my teeth
beetles in birch bark   my days
                    flew on feathered wings hunting needs
bones picked clean digesting seeds sweat

sipping dew
with pebbles lodged in the windpipe
my nights hummed with wasp flight
about the softened flesh of fallen fruit determined
to taste something sweet
blood –
rush through mushroom ears
and old ghosts shaped moss-mists with thumbs
my friend
was me and I was him as we peeked into one
another's core in a life
sped on
and spun
by acid winds of years held down and bottled up
as stars fell
around us tumbling
down the slopes
of this grim god's hill-home

when my body crawled
back to the path
lips cheeks brow stained
with purple juice
I was an old
silverbeard-man who had bound
his wild shadow but buried
his own true name.

Human Rubble

Trumans, London – dark greenish-brown,
perfect apart from the slim neck
snapped off in zoetrope mountain scape jags.
Gateshead and Leadgate circled
in pale mint bloom along the line
of a break more scoop than smash.
Six fluid ounces of Wards Orange Crush
as almost unscathed – its length
ribbed like a pleasuring sheath,
the bottom neatly lopped off
in perfect decapitation.
Berwick and a rampant lion furl
on a miniature spinnaker sail –
Gil, Trade on a bowed parallelogram.
The base of something, pressed into a dome
with only four numbers – one, three, seven, oh –
N & B on a thick chunk of polished molasses,
anagrams moulded into birthplace clues.
Porcelain offcut with plough dirtied hairlines
chattered through its delicate motifs
bears a message on its crepitated base –
Dianthus. Stoke on Tre

The Spring and the Lambs

The lambs tell me   I am   dead.
My feet no longer feel the press of grit into their   soles.
I notice they are   bare.
I am   risen.
Pliant sponge of moss between my toes – ten tines   plugging
the good of the   Earth.
I am   whole,
I am   unblemished.
I can hear the underground   world,
the gentle chafe of mole paws, busy spatulas   shifting
muck into a wonty-tump, poking out their   starry
noses. They have discovered   contentment
in blindness. They tell me about the   simplicity
of worms, how they are just   skin
and juice. A tree has sprung from the   welt
of green. It boughs me a dozen   fruits.
I am   gorging
on berries –   I am   hungry
for apple flesh. Angels cry me waterfalls of light – they   promise
life, life.   I am   everlasting,
it is written on bright foreheads –   *God! God! God!*

Crusoe Recycled

I left my eyes at the edge of the shore
Strung upon the skyline for any sign
Of help or hindrance or hope and hid
Myself safely within my grand designs
Among the precious salvage of the ship,
Keeping measurements of the weather
Tending my tasks and mechanics
(Bible and journal)
Mindful of my most loyal subjects
And the bare facts of our survival.

Each night the island sings its despair
Over the waves ever the wind
And parrots that call out my name
And the god of the goats dances,
Mortalled on my rum,
Across rocky mountain ledges
Teasing typhoons from clouds
Spinning the thunder of Gomorrah
With nimble fingers and cloven hoofs.

In the morning there are footprints
Everywhere, on the beach, the meadow,
Along the slats of my rope bridges – raw data:
Cannibals, tax inspectors, corrupt politicians
Having searched for me, their sovereign.
Slave I am to sudden bouts of hysteria brought
On by sunstroke, seaweed, a she-goat's smell,
Swarms of flies round the corpse of a gull.

To soothe my raw nerves I focus on The Job –
The sculptor of rough clay figurines;
Each one of them looks something like me
But a different colour - due to this earth,
I erect fences, cultivate gardens, burn them down
In games of all-out war and contrition.
The flames purify my figurines,
Reduce the contradictions to smudge,
All my dear children I name you Adam.

Some evenings when I roam
I expect to find something remarkable –
A pocket watch on a sand dune,
A black box bobbing in the bay's shallows
A dead i-phone overgrown by rushes
And wonder if I manufactured them myself
In a moment of genius-absent-mindedness
While fidgeting for Friday.

Every Saturday morning I stand
My children along the beach,
We build such marvellous sandcastles,
Palaces, cities inhabited by mermaids,
Springfield complete with a Homer and a Marge
As the high tide rolls in we all hold hands
To sing our hymn, "Castaways all – Get us out of here!"
Until we remember that the show is over,
Pulled mid-season. The celebrities scribbled
Some autographs and left, and we were eventually
Repatriated, although, it's hard to fit back in.
The long isolation is tattooed on my skin.

Crusoe Insane

HappyTalkyTalkyHappyTalkBoutFingsYooLakTooooDoooooo!
Snatchy song-snatch. Member, all youse wee likkle mud-men!
Youse too wee likkle to member ah had square-box yakk-o-vishun
goggle-eye once. *YouseGotsToHasADreeeeemIfYouseNotsGotsNoDreeeeeem!*

Comin' from it, collours, collours of the sky-bow – aye, belief it!
An'all them peopuls, ah swear, drissed lak them parrits 'ere, bluesan
redsan spanlgeyella. Beooootifuel wimmen lak you nivver sin.
Dissert Island me arse – nowt lak this shiteole. Whirsem? Whirsem eh?

Whirsem 'appy peopluls? Bild me ain outo squashclay – angryone,
sadone, fatone, thinone, prettyone, uglyone, bigmoothone. Smashem
whick-whack! Teachem to look at me, talkin hind me back.
Thinkah donnow? Ah eats good clamshell, bad clamshell – spews

me ringup sumtimes. No edducashions here 'cept learn by youse
mistaks. Fust tim ah come, ah split the sole o'me foot on a stonefish.
Now, I wears it lak a bleb, hugean rottin on the endo me leig. Ah stink
lak ulcers – think ahm slowlie gowin poisoned, proper mad.

YooIntNivverGonnaHavADreeeeemCumTru

Trinity

paper > rock
rock > scissors
scissors > paper

during autumn rains we watch for breaks in the clouds
i think o' the giants that came afore us
and those who'll one day come again

rumbling in thunder

and how we're mice scurrying between holes
whiskers twitching in sharp erratic jerks
o' determined survival gainst all odds

rock > scissors
scissors > paper
paper > rock

the singing bowls are brimming undra the leaks

what i L O V E D was the solidity o' wet sand
undra the foot then it's liquidification
as the pressure's released

the way the tidal sheen reflects
the spectacle o' the evenin' sky
the smooth grey voice o' the sea in a fossil

scissors > paper
paper > rock
rock > scissors

there must be others out there, somewhere

raindrops sizzle in the fire pytt
me body withers on the branch
i know o' no net that can catch the spirit

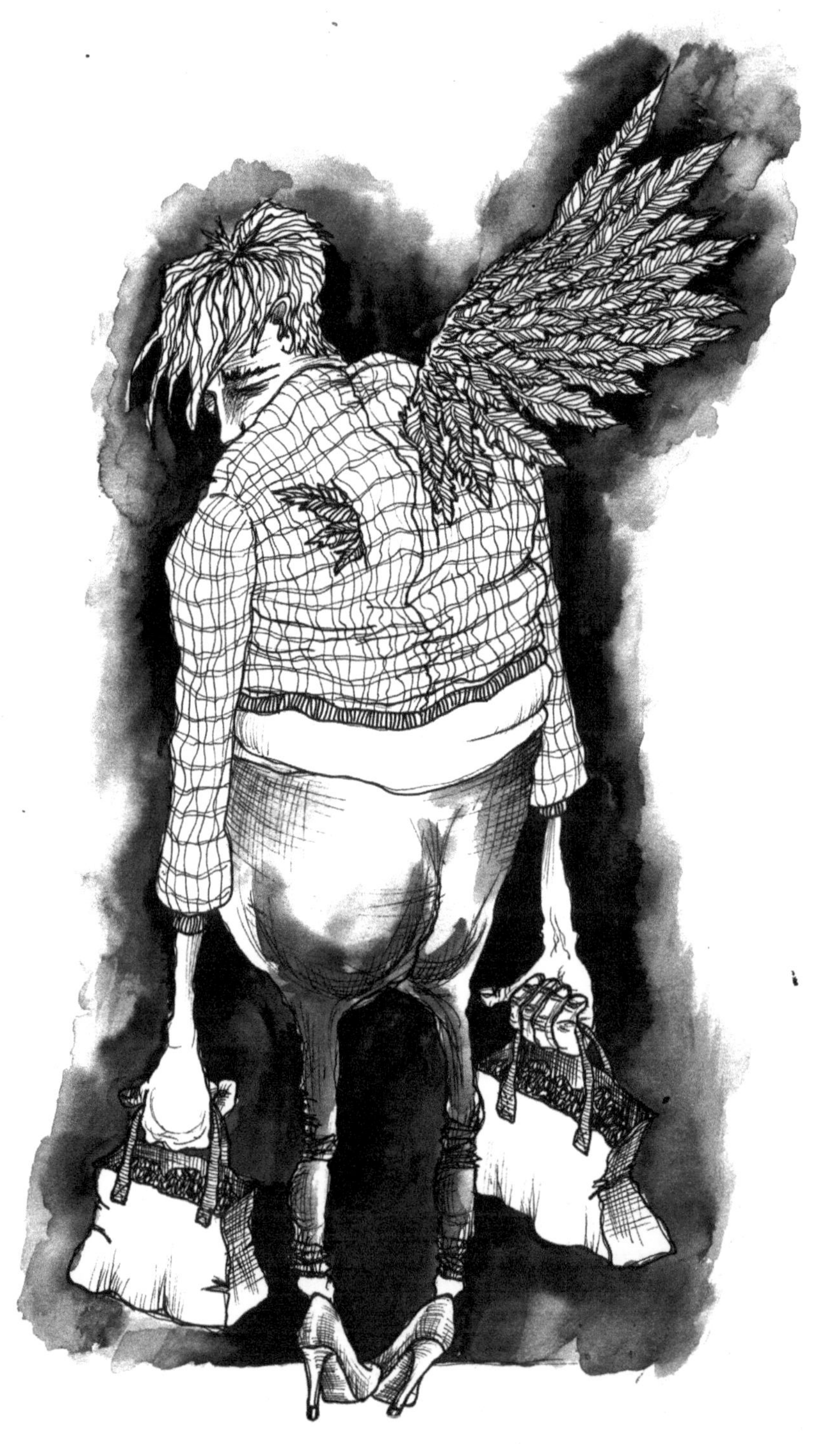

There is a Heaven

Centuries of humans wishing for one cannot have come to nothing.
Those prayers sent skyward should have built a bridge of faith
by now – we trap upon it, nimble as Gruff goats, above the troll.

The open arms of those we loved are waiting – I have seen them
buried with worms, their cold mud bones and powdered ash
gone to earth. I have wished them up a Shangri-la,

complete with gates, clouds like mallow butter. Wings,
strong and built with wraiths of feather. Flight, after years
of grounding, they slip their feet of clay, untether mortal coil.

We are moments – palm prints on windows, a fleet of leaves.
These angel-friends, they sigh me through the ozone,
tell me there will come a time for me to hear this raptured song.

Karma might have carved me to a hillock – hulled me of my charm
but heaven bides its time and waits to make me beautiful. A sylph,
whose sins remain below, corkindrills in the flame.

Escape

The Waiyhtless One cums afore the deer stir
while badgers snuffle leaves, grub black earth,
whispers, *The May-Bride has died in childbirth!*
She breaks me spellbonds with a crow feather
drags me from me pallet, bids me follow her –
'though we both know it may trigger THE DEARTH.
She hisses a questyon, *What is your life worth?*
wi' a finger n' thumb she plucks one hair
from me head, blows it into the chill niyht air.
She turns me t'ward the dark river's reed-beds
shoves me hard, n' spits, *Go now, find somewhere*
you can hide safe afore the death-news spreads.
On feet that have forgotten how te walk
I stumble, limp; hear her call like a hawk.

Moon Lore

Three knots in a rope. Zephyr, blinter, doister –
witch's breath, coughed into bowline, reef and hitch.
Purga from my open throat, hoar on my tongue to soothe
waves or sunder them, raise devils in grains from the shore.

My lullaby is wet in my mouth – I nurse a gosling storm
to my breast in place of a child. *Come, sailors!* My psalms
are bamboozlement, lyrics to weave them moonlight, sing
them bights of magic. Cilophyte, I. They see my woman's

half, rising o'er the tide, see globed tits, round and bumped
as an echinoid shell, lanterns hard to the air, hard to the promise
of lip and thumb. I can make them forgetful – they cannot see
my tendril legs, eight feelers, curling, uncurling beneath,

testing the weight of water, working out whether I want
to be tender or terrible, whether I might love them
or dash them to rock. Come to my octopus embrace, come
to deep, come to me and be lost to the world on top.

Witch Watters

Spread between bridges
midniyht on the polished river
singing the song o' the tide

steel in a two-faced wind
a train graveyard
and the town's inverted twin

spore clouds o' smoke
from mushroom chimneys
bloom inte commedia masks
deaths heads, ink caps.

Sing back te it –
a lullaby o' brick dust n' bone-
soft vowel sounds, sibilance.

Upriver the channel
seems te split where it doesn't –

for more than a moment
I don't recall
which way I've come.

Haruspex

Outside are the dogs Revelation 22:14-15

The fable is I want 'em for my thirst, to slip their juices
down the dryness of my throat. Grapes! We do not eat 'em,
Aesop – you are ill-informed. Foxes glean no sustenance
from fruit, fool. But meat! Blood and guts, gristle in the gaps
between my teeth, gnash and gobble, rip and tear. Here
is the trick – in the entrails are the fortunes of the world.
They tell a tortile tale – each crimp, each corkscrew kink
a message from the dead. These vitals have their opinions.

Your end is coming – outside are the dogs!
You, with your wizard's mind – God has no truck
with you. A sin to grovel so, amongst the giblets
of the dammed! As if whispers in prairie oysters
can communicate the whim of fate! For shame,
you copper-carrot divvil – a hail of stones for you.
When the clouds next piss their sleet and snow,
may you be smitten with rock – be pebbledashed.

Extispicy! Religion hates magicians. Silence, bowels!
Everyone has swallowed secrets. I can taste them, sweet
and bitter in the bile – the dandelions they ate, the love
they made, behind each other's backs. *Loaves to fishes?*
Water, wine? His miracles seem a conjurers trick to me –
did he answer your coughed up prayers any more
than necromancers, doomed to the sulphur? Any more
than I can divine a lifetime, see a soul in livers?

The Long Walkers

This was no dream
though a cataract white
misted my view of this morning's street,

Curtains drawn
to hoard stubborn pools
of nightfall in dormant living rooms.

A sore throat stung
at each swallow, as I trudged
the length of the terraced row

Off to the newsagents
around the corner, slowly
as if meeting an executioner.

My head a mish-mash
of lingering dreams, crows
erupted from a yawn's silent scream.

Joining a ragged line
of shadow men, one or two
nodded but said nothing when

I slipped between
them into position, the lives
behind us difficult to discern:

Safe homes, the soft folds
of lovers, laughing-tearful
bairns tucked up under covers.

Some of us kept birds
in the weave of their beards, others
wore slighted hearts on their sleeves

Some limped with each step,
some hummed a frayed thread
from the rag-end of a tune, or drummed

Out a rhythm with slaps
on the back of the strider
in front, to take up any slack

With our shoulders
hunched against the rain,
we sing how all but the road is foreign.

Following the trails
that twist through hills,
in woods of green oak, ash and birch

Traipse what-once-were
fields, the edge of sheer cliffs,
and nap in a ditch by a sheltering hedge

Sometimes we mull
on the imagined beast we're tracking:
a flash of pale fur, its claws and its teeth

The shimmer of its scales,
its feathers, horn, its glorious comb
or the dread behind us, shadowing

All thought of the day
when we waste it, when we're allowed
to return, each one of us wearing its face.

Island of Kings

Revelation 17:3 I saw a woman sit upon a scarlet coloured beast. 17:9 The seven heads are seven mountains, on which the woman sitteth 2:22 I will throw her onto a sickbed

A Divinity of Piss-Beards – under bristles sleeps a silken kid, begging
to be palmed. Their breath is grass, tells a tale of springtime meadow.
The King of Them, he ate me from the bottom up, ate away the clothes
I wore – made spaghetti of the threads. I felt his rabbits cleft – he calmly

took my skin in peels of pain and all the time, his two-pronged touch.
I felt him walk my ledges, deft on sides of breast – a trip of halven prints,
bracts where he burst me underneath. 'Tis only clumsy ones that fall –
for them, the scree. I begged for cud from his tongue, sweet as liar's candy,

fingered stairways up the ridges of his horns. Above me nodding heavy
with such weight of crown, his splendid head. I was hulked by your rutting,
God of the Wild! Held in hocks snapped as elbow crooks, weighted under
kindling ribs, I made a body-bridge under his touch, all flex and rise.

Slave as I was to the rough of his fur, he left me blistered – raspberries
bloomed his path, rashed my chin with mustachio scratch. Passion in the hay,
in mattress sweat where I lay, shit and farm smell – after, counting goblins
in corners, gathering dark to the back of my eyes. You sang me nothing, Pan,

but gasps to settle frost across the plough of me – I am Babylon's Whore.
I saw a woman sit upon a scarlet coloured beast. I rode him, sat on
seven mountains, sucked on seven heads. I fucked a Satyr, I was ruined,
Dabih – how apt your constellations! Island of Kings! I looked to their irides,

looked for semblance of soul – they blinked me comfits, jellied in glass.
Tawny marmalade spark, firebolt flashes of older knowledge – we are cornucopia
in your hands. Eat us, drink us – make thou merry 'pon us, rage of Revelation
coughed in musky breaths. *Beware*, they bleat from mountain tops.

We throw such Jezebels on our beds! All these piseogs! *Pluck the wrong petal,*
and he loves you not! Great He-Goat, laughing down from Goya's wall,
his witches tame – philtre in their veins, eyes all saucers of milk. He will
leave them, lapped out dowdies – He will litter the pit with their shells.

The Hours of the Virgin

Matins

I remember when I was untouched but ached to be.
I remember unloveliness – shorn hair, crossed teeth.
How do you be beautiful? *Dear God, if I am good*
will you give me plaits? When I wake up,
could I please have pretty dresses?

Lauds

My eyes are open. I have brought to end this vigil for better things.
They have not come – I woke the same. Same little belly rolls,
hair on my arms, same fingers – the times the other girls let me try
their rings they never fit. They have little signet rings of gold,
some even have initials – curly *L's* or *R's*. How I want one!
How do you get those boys to hold your hand at parties?
I am sick of minding the coats.

Prime

Dear God – my friend has a rag-doll. It has calico skin.
I imagine I am sewn with love. A face, planted with hyacinth
eyes and rosebud lips. How do I grow these things? I listen
for a heartbeat in the stuffing. Something so lovely must surely
be alive. How does she stay so still?

Terce

I want to sing! Like a bird with a throat full of bubbles I want to tell
the world I pushed my breast on a thorn. It broke my skin. I learned
how it felt to touch a wolf. I learned about blood. How long does it hurt?

Sext

I learned to be slim – I learned how to look good in jeans.
I had an affair with dancing – I kissed the rims of glasses,
sucked from cigarettes and blew hot smoke into faces
that seemed to want to listen to my conversation.

None

This must be it because it is my wedding day – I am acres of taffeta,
I am borne aisle-wards in my bodice, crushed among the pearls.
My father holds my arm – we steady each other. If I had known
that this was the last time we would have been together, arm in arm
I would have walked us up and down and up and down until
I had memorised the way his arm felt under my hand. I would
have paid more attention to the way age made him frailer,
took his dad-smell more acutely to my brain.

Vespers

I am dwindling. My baby is as tall as me now, almost,
each *mammy* is the chiming of the clearest cow-bell.
My heart is full of him, full for him – if I could feel
out a perfect life for him I would, if only I could feel
away all future pain. I do not want to die – how do I
imagine being anywhere without him?

Compline

Sometimes your mother is never going to love you. Trying to understand
the reasons why will use up decades of your life. My husband is a stranger.
You used to smile all the time, he tells me and because of all the years
we shared I look the other way; wait to end my life as barren as I began.

Graeae

Listen!
Something skew-wiff approaches from stage left.
Pass me our eye Sister, so that I may spy.
Is it a man? He may fall for me, for one of us!
Take us from this grey world into a realm of love.
Tch, that time has long gone, Sister, if ever it was here
faded by the time it flourished, my dear.

What are we, Sister? I have forgotten.

They called us Widows of Perpetual War
but I don't recall any husband in my past's shards.

And what have we become?
We are rags and bones my Sister, figurine in exile.
We are rocks, sand and surf. We are vermin
scratching at the threshold of order, sleeping
within the hollow of a blown tern egg, watching
menopausal waves swell beyond the scar;
two whole months of blood.

Where are we, Sis? Kiss me, pass over our slug
tongue so I may taste the tremors of this place
where Orpheus sings sad songs of loss, where we squat
in the charnel reek of the deep cave mouth.
Hand me our snaggle tooth, Sister, so I can chew
this gristle, strip off fat, scrape skin and sinew.

Sister, sisters, what shall we become?
Gymnasts, my sweet, with perfect balance, tight-roping
the borders with the grace of cirrus uncinus.
We shall blow pink bubbles with chewing gum –
mine shall be the biggest. No, mine will be the best!

What must we do, my Sisters?
Draw old pacts in damp sand with picked clean bones.
Scrape the silver from the moon. Pass me the eye, Sister,
the one we stole from a stranger. We must decipher
the monologic view, refract it's gaze in water prisms;
weave wyrd threads between ante-life and after-life,
skate around the frozen sea, wait for the blood to stop.

Lodging With Old Mother Rust

i)

The hands are stuck at half past two,
skewering time like a rare insect
in the collector's glass display case –

Memories diced by a serrated kitchen knife
in a tumbledown shack in the woods,
the women, her daughters, peel

the skins off pale moments, remove the eyes
let each one drop into an enamelled bowl,
soft, wet plops accompany gossip of bairns

and blokes and poor old Prometheus,
the fire and all of the things it can do.

ii)

One woman smiles, holding onto her future.
When she was younger they called her Skinny
Skinny Minney, will never own a pinny.

These days she couldn't give a hoot, she's noticed
how years seep across the tarnished mirror,
slicing one for the pan against her thumb.

She once made love in a cornfield
beneath buzzing pylons, in the setting sun
beside railway tracks curved into the world.

That's how she likes to remember it.

iii)

Goods trains grumble all through the night,
in the pitch of the mine timber props creak,
men-moles groan, listening for the creep
as loaded wagons of Blue Billy roll.

There's a needle in a drawer to sew today
onto tomorrow, another to bind a love spell,
coppers in a jam jar, potcheen in the still.

Above the canopy a steel bird with a lion's roar
scours a straight edge across the brazen sky
that hammers the whole land flat.

iv)

Just last washday, on account of the war,
the town square was stripped of its railings.
Soon they'll be calling for her thimbles.

Through the visor in the blast furnace
alchemy shines like the birth of a new star,
heat turns all thought to cinders.

Barbed wire tangles keep some out, some in.
One slug rests in a chamber of a killing machine
(a one in six chance of blowing your brains out)

dangerous drinking games to pass the time
on long winter nights when the crazies come.

The Art of Forgetting

(After Jannis Kounellis)

The chairs would like to watch the pantomime of black coats.
(Yes they do, oh, yes they do! – Oh, no they don't!)
Watch their ritual dance upon the wall, absent of bodies
In a vacant enactment of commerce with nothing left to gain -
As flat and alien as a soundless Super 8 projection's flicker
Of some ancient family gathering you choose not to remember;
(No you don't! Oh, yes you do! No you don't!) –
Mothballs and the texture of the heavy weave on your neck-
Thirteen coats of gentlemen who shook hands in agreement
Took the path of the handlebar moustache, set their jaws,
Filled their pockets, made a stand, played the pantomime
Of pennies, guineas and pounds with stiff upper lips.
The chairs would like to watch the parade of black coats
But they have been shrouded in mourning sheets
(Yes they have, they have! – Oh, no they've not!)
Those thirteen gentlemen are long gone and their coats
Retreat behind a waterfall of semi-precious myth.

www.ingramcontent.com/pod-product-compliance
Lightning Source LLC
LaVergne TN
LVHW060627110826
845147LV00015B/953

9781912211357